Advance Praise for *Step Up Now*

"An insightful, accessible, and comprehensive approach to achieving optimal wellness, influence, and personal fulfillment."

STEPHEN A. STUMPF
Professor of Management and the Fred J. Springer Chair in Business Leadership, Villanova University Faculty, Wharton Executive Education, Philadelphia, PA

"*Step Up Now* is a compelling and provocative book, filled with smart questions and interesting examples that engage the reader. The prose achieves a magical combination of sound wisdom and fun reading. It synthesizes the fundamentals of sound leadership that are not often expressed in traditional books on the subject. Business leaders walk away with an important perspective that is critical for effective and sustainable leadership in these times."

PEGGY L. DASILVA
Senior Executive, Real estate industry, New York, NY

"Susan Freeman is truly a talented and engaging writer. She has composed a very practical and concise playbook for leaders while at the same time maintaining a conversational writing style that disarms the reader and challenges them to consider a broad array of leadership influences. Susan's winsome coaching style is evident throughout the book and each chapter reinforces a feeling that you are in a personal coaching session with the author herself."

DEREK ROBERTS
CEO, Integrity Solutions, Phoenix, AZ

"As a partner in a firm that oversees investments in 50 small businesses, it is easy to see the tremendous value of these simple, yet powerful processes and approaches to self-knowledge and leadership. Ms. Freeman does an exceptional job of translating Eastern ways of thinking to transforming Western business practices. There is much wisdom here. Her simple, yet powerful advice, questions, and exercises provide tools to think about business challenges and opportunities in new and different ways. While the types of change in mind and body she advocates require discipline and hard work, the rewards are commensurate. I cannot think of a single leader in any of our businesses that could not meaningfully benefit from reading this book."

STEVEN SWARTZMAN
Partner, C3 Capital, LLC, Kansas City, MO

"*Step Up Now* is easy-to-read, inspirational and rich in tools to help reflection. Each subject, from how to design conversations or to recognize the impact of moods and emotions, offers an opportunity to learn and identify their importance to leaders. This book enables the self-generating capacity of readers to take steps towards achieving integrated leadership."

ROSY TORRIANI
*Director, Organization Development for Europe, Middle East and Africa
Fortune 50 Company, Switzerland*

"*Step Up Now* is a gift of how to be present, inspired and consciously-empowered to professionally ascend to where we want to be with others. It permits us to quickly take a moment to reflect. To dream. To breathe. To become centered. To see ourselves, others and opportunities with greater awareness and from a new perspective. To mindfully move forward, with thoughtful, easy-to-do actions that allow us to *Step Up Now*. The title's initials appropriately spell SUN. Perhaps, symbolic of finding our inner light and personal quest. The trip is meant to be joyful. For me, it's just begun. Thank you."

TERRY FRISHMAN
Owner, Creative Marketing Workshops, Teacher at three culinary schools, New York, NY

"*Step Up Now*" is a clear and direct approach to improving leadership skills. It offers definitive action plans, clear examples and no nonsense commentary on regular practices that can be successfully employed in leadership. As the author states, it demonstrates 'learning to use all of ourselves' to achieve results. The book opens your mind to ask pertinent questions, to search for answers and to use the knowledge to better ourselves and our environment."

MARIA ARNONE, MCC
Founder and President, The Learning Partnership, New York, NY

"A must read for anyone in leadership! The crisis of our time requires a different approach to leadership at all levels. *Step Up Now* will show you how to build trust and loyalty in all of your relationships, including the relationship with yourself."

TOM JOSEPH IYOOB
Former CEO of Newfield Network, Founder, Summit Personal Development
Boulder, CO

"Finally, a book that clearly connects what a leader does and who the leader is in a holistic sense: mind, body and spirit. Taken seriously, *Step Up Now* creates a deep self-awareness that opens a world of new opportunities and enables leaders to embrace the change we find all around us with a positive, 'let's go conquer it' spirit. As a management consultant, I have seen first-hand the power of the principles Susan Freeman so clearly articulates. *Step Up Now* is a thought-provoker from beginning to end."

BARBARA ANN BLUE

President, Business Performance Group, Inc., Former Chair of Leadership, Florida

"As a CEO of several biotech companies in the last 20 years, I have found that adaptability and the ability to influence others are prerequisites to effective leadership. This is critical in the fluid environment created by changes in technology, regulations and global market dynamics. Susan Freeman's *Step Up Now* provides a refreshing, holistic approach to increasing one's ability to inspire others. By breaking down walls in communication, opening oneself to novel ideas and ambiguous situations, sharpening one's vision by centering around core values, we can improve leadership success, while enjoying less stress and better physical health."

WINNIE H. WAN, PhD

Executive Chair and CEO, OncoHealth Corp., San Jose, CA

"Susan Freeman has mastered the skill of developing the 'right' questions and models this mastery in her book. In my many years of experience in teaching and coaching, the value of the question posed cannot be underestimated. It is the catalyst for changing mindsets."

CORINNE B. YOUNG, PhD

Senior Partner, The Worldwide Change Group
Professor of Responsible Leadership, The University for Peace, Costa Rica

"*Step Up Now* contains a simple, yet powerful message. As COO of an 8,000 employee organization, the lessons in this book offer a valuable perspective on the often missing ingredient of organizational effectiveness. Being able to communicate simply and effectively at all levels of an organization is critical. Understanding the connection between care and commitment helped me to reshape communications and create more passionate goals. Consciously shifting from automatic to intentional thought has helped me avoid reacting immediately to ideas without taking time to process. There are lessons here for everyone willing to invest just a little time for their future."

JOHN TOMLIN
Chief Operating Officer, The Auto Club Group, Tampa, FL and Detroit, MI

"As a young emerging leader, *Step Up Now* demonstrated that I have already chosen to repeat patterns that keep me small and unfocused. I learned how to identify my larger vision, my real passions, and I am taking action now to execute my dreams for an unprecedented future.

"Susan Freeman creates an arena for people to shift out of fear and autopilot into a new decision-making pattern that utilizes intuition and real passions. *Step Up Now* awakens our true values and teaches the precious reminder that we are always *at choice*. The freedom of choice allows for a shift in action that facilitates change and brings us closer to happiness and closer to life.

Step Up Now is a book of self-awareness with clearly actionable ways to create a new path to excellence."

CAROLINE YOUNG
Director of Product, Rivet Games, Inc., San Francisco, CA

"*Step Up Now* is a wonderful combination of East meets West business philosophy that I am sure to use on a day to day basis. In my role as a leader of an organization with 1,000 employees, I found the short case studies followed by personal action items to be an invaluable tool for any busy executive. I must note that I find the action items, which I will utilize in both my personal and professional life, as a resource that makes this a must read throughout any business organization."

SANDIP I. PATEL,
Chief Administrative Officer and General Counsel,
Universal Health Care Group, Inc., St. Petersburg, FL

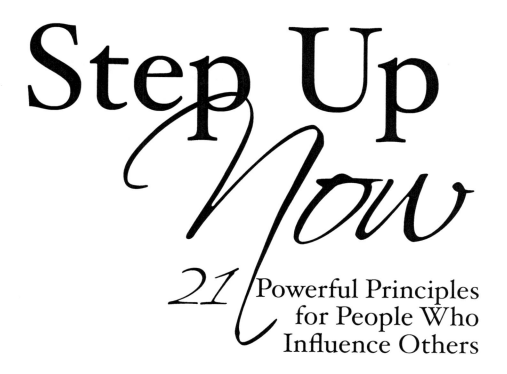

Step Up Now

21 Powerful Principles for People Who Influence Others

How to joyfully create your authentic pathway to influencing others and getting breakthrough results

SUSAN S. FREEMAN

Love Your Life

Love Your Life Publishing
7127 Mexico Road Suite 121
St. Peters, MO 63346
www.loveyourlifepublishing.com

ISBN: 978-1-934509-47-0
Library of Congress Control Number: 2011944903

Printed in the United States of America
First Printing 2012
Cover and internal design: www.Cyanotype.ca
Editing by Gwen Hoffnagle

Author Contact:
Susan S. Freeman
Susan@StepUpLeader.com
www.StepUpLeader.Com
813-962-0042

Warning – Disclaimer

The purpose of this book is to educate and entertain. The author and/or publisher do not guarantee that anyone following these techniques, suggestions, tips, ideas, or strategies will become successful. The author and/or publisher shall have neither liability nor responsibility to anyone with respect to any loss or damage caused, or alleged to be caused, directly or indirectly, by the information contained in this book.

Dedication

For Tom, Danny, Andy, and Jonathan:

You bring constant joy, surprise, meaning, and love to my life. Thank you for always reminding me that the only thing we are in charge of is ourselves.

Acknowledgements

I would like to acknowledge a few people without whom this book would not have happened:

Stephen A. Stumpf, Professor of Management and Fred J. Springer Chair in Business Leadership, Villanova University, and Faculty, Wharton Executive Education, who was my first real teacher of leadership and whose friendship and support throughout my career have been invaluable.

Maria Arnone, Founder, The Learning Partnership, whose mentoring, friendship, and gentle nudges have been a blessing over the years.

Julio Olalla, Founder of the Newfield Network, and coach extraordinaire, as well as all the staff and mentor coaches at Newfield who opened my eyes and helped me develop capacity for this magnificent work.

Tina Crumpacker, of TMC Productions, for being willing to take a stand for me and for world transformation in an impactful way.

Lynne Klippel, whose knowledge, wisdom, and wit about books helped me birth this project.

Donna Kozik, whose enthusiastic commitment to helping others write their books inspired me to put what I know into a book, while having fun in the process.

Birgit Zacher-Hanson, for creative and generous collaboration as a colleague.

Yogi Amrit Desai and the Amrit Institute for bringing forth priceless, timeless universal wisdom and making it accessible to the western world.

My parents, Howard Swartzman and Lea Endlich, whose unconditional love is a source of my strength.

My clients, who have taught me so much and trusted me with their inner and outer worlds.

My husband, Tom, and sons Danny, Andy, and Jonathan, for being willing to put up with what it took for me to learn the lessons in this book so I could share them with others.

Special thanks to Jonathan, my youngest son and poet extraordinaire, for allowing me to borrow his beautiful poems as inspiration for the book's message.

About the Author

Susan S. Freeman, MBA, NCC, ACC
Executive Success Strategist

Susan S. Freeman is Founder of Step Up Leader and author of *Step Up Now: 21 Powerful Principles for People Who Influence Others.* "What I do best is help entrepreneurial leaders break through their barriers and create extraordinary professional and personal results. My specialty is excavating the brilliant, knowing leader inside of you. I am known for transforming difficult challenges into soul-satisfying solutions. I help leaders leave a legacy of which they can be proud."

Susan's unique gift is the integration of western corporate and entrepreneurial work experience with ancient eastern wisdom traditions. Her business background is extensive and diverse, including corporate strategic marketing in London and New York, founder and leader of a unique non-profit enterprise, and vice-president of a boutique executive search firm.

Her work weaves through the mind, body, and emotions, where the seat of leadership lives. She combines the rigors of diverse business expertise with presence, creativity, and intuition for the sake of helping clients achieve breakthrough results. Susan truly understands the requisite skills and pressures faced by leaders today. She has the background to boldly challenge clients, while keeping it safe enough for them to explore new possibilities.

Susan earned her MBA from Columbia University and her BA from Wellesley College. She received her coach training and certification from The Newfield Network. Susan is an accredited coach with the International Coach Federation, as well as an MSP-certified business facilitator.

She believes that "today's organizational climate and leadership challenges require an entirely different framework than at any other time in human history. Organizations will either thrive or struggle depending upon the ability of leaders to introduce conversations of meaning and authenticity to the workplace. Discretionary effort, loyalty, and exceptional performance result from engaged and empowered individuals and teams. We must connect our hearts and heads in service to a deeper purpose and sense of mission. In so doing, we transform ourselves, our organizations, and our world, experiencing the joy that comes from purposeful living."

Susan is a lifelong learner, with over fifteen years of study and practice in transformational human potential, mindfulness, yoga, and wellness. Her passion is helping transform the world one leadership conversation at a time. Susan is married and has three grown sons. Rarely a day goes by when she doesn't reach for a piece of dark chocolate.

Is This Book for You?

Are you a person who is in a position to influence others yet feel disempowered and can't figure out why and what to do about it?

You may be frustrated because you are in an especially challenging situation at work, having problematic relationships with colleagues and others. All you want to do is fix "it!" You know there has to be something different, but have tried everything you know.

What if it isn't about the actions? What if there is something surprising that has even greater influence on outcomes and results?

What I do is help entrepreneurial leaders break through their barriers to extraordinary professional and personal results.

The way I do this is through whole system learning, tapping into the innate wisdom already available to all of us but seldom utilized. The reason I can do this is because I care deeply and passionately about the state of our world and the people in it. The way I know how to influence and affect change is one person, one conversation, one group at a time. My approach to obtaining breakthrough results uniquely weaves through the mind, the heart, and the authentic self. I combine the rigors of diverse business expertise with presence, creativity, and intuition for the sake of helping clients become extraordinary. I boldly challenge my clients, while keeping it safe for them to explore new possibilities.

Based upon the latest research in emotional intelligence, neuroscience, ancient wisdom, and personal practice, this book is for you IF:

You have an inner drive to be a *learner*. You have curiosity and desire to learn more. You strive to dive deeper. You are a person who influences others.

———◆———

If this book influenced you, I would enjoy hearing about it. Drop me an e-mail at Susan@StepUpLeader.com or on the web at www.StepUpLeader.com

Contents

Foreword

―――――

"Stop. Look. Listen." Advice I often heard from my mom in preparation for crossing a street. Those days are gone. Today I rarely stop and barely glance. As for listening, it is more likely to be to my own thoughts or an iPod – certainly not to the multitude of messages available in my environment. Yet I survive and prosper. Sometimes this is enough. Other times I have a desire to influence that environment and those in it; to feel a greater sense of meaningfulness, competence, and progress in what I do. *Step Up Now* is for those who want more of the intrinsic rewards associated with what they do – a stronger sense of influence, meaningfulness, competence, and progress. If you want these rewards, read on.

The *Step Up Now* principles provide clear guidance for actions which will stop you from "doing what you've always done and getting what you've always got." These principles, like the spokes on a wheel, connect your hub to the outcomes you desire. They provide leverage. They create synergy from your actions. And much like spokes on a wheel, a few stronger spokes serve as well as many weaker spokes. Each principle adds value, but all are not required all the time. Personally, Underlying Conversations, Power of Stopping, Authenticity, and Attitude of Gratitude have become my core spokes – my new habits. Other principles guide me. All reflect scientific learnings of the past decade and the hard-earned wisdom of the author. For those willing to pause (stopping may still be too difficult) and trust the process, these rewards will soon follow.

—STEPHEN A. STUMPF,
Professor of Management and the Fred J. Springer Chair in Business Leadership,
Villanova University, and Faculty, Wharton Executive Education, Philadelphia, Pennsylvania

Preface

———◆———

I arrived at my life's work by a circuitous route, but I truly believe that all the other aspects of my professional life have helped shape and inform my uniqueness and strength as a transformational coach.

I was a psychology major in college, and was always curious about what makes us tick. In the last decade, I have come to appreciate that traditional psychology has as its premise the "self." The focus is therefore on the present and on keeping the "self" intact. Think of it as maintenance. What captures my interest now is transformative human learning that promotes change and evolution. The focus is not to maintain the status quo, but rather to allow organic movement toward a more productive and joyful life that is integrated and whole. Never did I imagine that helping people who influence others in this way would become my life's work.

My entire professional life has been in the business and organizational arena. After graduate school, I worked on Madison Avenue in strategic marketing and advertising for the world's largest consumer packaged-goods companies. On moving to Tampa, I founded a Florida affiliate of a national non-profit organization (now in its twenty-first year) dedicated to increasing business investment in the arts and culture of my community. That led to my own consulting firm, offering leadership training and development to organizational and non-profit board leaders. Later, I joined a boutique firm specializing in retained executive search for clients seeking A-caliber senior executives, while helping build the marketing and branding platform for the company.

Seven years into that role, I began to experience uneasiness about continuing in the profession. I enjoyed the work, but felt a pull toward something not yet identifiable. I saw that for many of their problems, clients needed the kind of help that could not be provided through a search placement. There were issues underneath the call for new leaders, including both leadership and culture. I felt frustrated that there was so much more to be done, yet I was not in a position to fulfill that need.

One day I received a call from a corporate recruiter for a large multi-national search firm. They were recruiting me for a senior level position with their firm's local office in Florida. After an initial round of talks locally, I was flown to Toronto for a full day of interviews. When offered the role, everyone was excited – that is, everyone but me.

There was a gnawing pit in my stomach. Something wasn't right, though because the economy was in a downward spiral and the offer was very attractive financially, it was the next logical step in my career. When called to ask if I was going to accept the offer on the spot, I blurted out "No." I was shocked at how forcefully and easily it came out. However, while that was easy, the next step of the journey proved to be much more difficult. If not this, then what? What was it that I really wanted to do with the rest of my life?

It is now apparent that what I thought was a crisis was really the beginning of a metamorphosis. I felt unease and uncertainty. After all, I was supposed to be the pro in this arena. People were coming to me for career guidance, yet I had no idea what to do for myself. I stewed around in this for many months, and finally took action. I hired a coach.

This simple act of committing to a different future was a powerful move. The coach supported me in an extensive process to discover my dream job. Several months after completing that process, my dream job unfolded. Much to my surprise, it was professional coaching.

I coach because I am most passionate about helping others discover their highest human potential for both performance *and* satisfaction. As a coach, I truly become more of who I am. I coach because I get excited about all the possibilities from the learning. I coach because I love breakthrough results that surpass expectations. I coach because I think it is one of the greatest gifts we can offer – the gift of our presence to another. It is so simple, yet so profound.

The inspiration for this book comes from my listening and learning as a coach. I hope that the principles found in these pages speak to you, inspire you, and motivate you to transform your being and doing, and ultimately how you influence and lead others. Our world depends on your doing so.

Introduction

"The heart says 'I am everything.' Wisdom says 'I am nothing.'
And in between is where I live."
—Susan S. Freeman

You feel it, don't you? The world is changing rapidly and profoundly. We are stretched beyond our capacity to do what we have always done. You know you are part of this, yet you may not know what to do about it.

Every aspect of the world is experiencing upheaval. Institutions, economies, and organizational structures are becoming obsolete, decaying, or dying. With what will they be replaced, and by whom?

If this question intrigues you, you are not alone. I believe it has never been more relevant for people who influence others, because you are on the front line of this transformation. Creating a brighter future for organizations that impact lives is in your hands.

This book is written for you – a busy person who influences others. It is written for people who lead in many ways, both large and small. It is not important how many people you influence, but that you *do* influence. You don't have a lot of time. You are bombarded with must-read information daily. Instead, you want no-nonsense material that satisfies your urge for learning a new way. You want to navigate the sea of transformation, and want a compass that's up to the task.

The contents of this book represent the lessons of my life and work. I offer them to you as a gift. They are written as a learning framework. They represent a multi-disciplinary, integrated approach gleaned over many years. I combine the language and experience of business with the wisdom from the East. My hope is to provide you with the fuel to make big shifts that are simple, yet profoundly effective.

I include multiple ways of delivering material, relying heavily on experiential and do-it-now learning, because these are the gateways to change. What do you remember better – riding a bike or doing geometry? Likely riding a bike, because you learned it in your entire body. It was *embodied*, while the geometry was learned only cognitively. The exercises in this book are designed to help you both learn and embody new concepts *and* new ways of being.

Why the urgency? At no time in history have there been shifts of the magnitude and pace as those we are experiencing in these times. Technology, especially the internet and cellular communication, has accelerated this shift. We are now connected globally and 24/7 through technology. But we are and always have been connected in another fundamental way, and that is through shared energy.

Quantum physics has helped connect cutting-edge science with timeless spirituality. Learning can and does take place in the non-physical domain. We now realize that energy is the field that unites us, that it is shared, and that *we* can affect it. In fact, it is probably the most powerful tool we have.

Because Western tradition precludes attention to the field of energy, we experience a lot of struggle. In our society it shows up as disconnection, feeling overwhelmed, stress, anxiety, depression, frustration, anger, and sometimes rage. The entrenched patterns and outmoded ways of thinking are predictable and comfortable for us, in spite of the fact that they cause undesirable results and, often, suffering.

There *is* a choice. Although it is easier to retain the old ways of thinking rather than embrace change, it is far less satisfying. I believe our inherent evolutionary drive as humans will serve to great advantage. The first step is to acknowledge that we simply *must* adapt to new ways. In order to *act* differently, we must *think* differently. It has never been more important to do so than now.

When I say new ways, I actually mean old. Very old. The wisdom in this book is actually ancient. The truths upon which these principles are based have been known for centuries. Yet as history progressed, we became so captivated with progress that we embraced the "duality divide," – man was declared a thinking, cognitive being, separate and distinct from the body, emotions, and nature itself.

Descartes exemplified this thinking during the Scientific Revolution in the famous quote: "I think, therefore I am." This became the rallying cry of the modern age. This philosophy provided the fertile ground for rigorous scientific thinking and experimentation. Logic ruled. Anything that couldn't be proven wasn't worth knowing.

Operating as if prediction and control are the end game has led to limitations. It is now understood that thinking (as dominated by the left-brain hemisphere), in the logical, concrete, and fact-based arena, is only *part* of what is necessary to thrive in modern times. We also need the right-brain, creative, synthetic, imaginative, intuitive part of human capacity. In fact there are some who believe this thinking is actually *the* set of skills for The Conceptual Age – the era we have entered. (*A Whole New Mind: Why Right-Brainers Will Rule the Future,* Daniel Pink, 2006*)*

Today's world sorely needs transformation rather than maintenance. Most people suffer from a modern affliction known as chronic stress. It has become so ingrained that many people suffer from less-than-optimal health and functionality at one end of the spectrum, while at the other end they are robbed of a full experience of life lived in the moment – a joy that is the human birthright. This affects every single one of us, and therefore impacts our organizational world profoundly.

I believe our organizations and institutions are at a breaking point. Old ways of operating and leading are insufficient for the twenty-first century. It begins with you. You lead and manage. As you grow, the work you do and the way you do it will evolve to better serve others. My dream is that as you make yourself better, you will make your team and organization better. We *need* better organizations – ones that truly serve. And service is an *inside* job.

This book is designed to help you develop awareness and the capacity to transform the way you see, work, and live. Through stories, case studies, and simple do-it-now exercises, you will learn the secrets of true influence. As you strengthen and deepen your capacity for self-mastery, so will you extend your influence. As you change, you change the world.

I invite you to Step Up Now.

———◆———

As a special free reader bonus, I have prepared a Step Up Leader Action Guide to accompany this book. It will assist you in getting the most out of the exercises. To obtain it, simply visit www.StepUpLeader.com and click on "Action Guide."

Redefined

The days of our lives are transient rhymes-
Not failed tunnels through formless time.
But sublime martyrs for lines uncrossed-
Cowards embossed by the luster of Life's shine.
We seem content with weekly checks
And a cheap bottle of wine-
Our days defined by someone else's enslaved brain,
Shackled with the weight of dreams denied-
(Just tattered seams, misunderstood-
We would fly if we could.)

So liberate your mind and
Lose yourself in realms redefined-
No more self-medication
Through prisons prescribed-
And static skies show new signs of Life, of
Beauty immersed in Poetry-
And Time-

We are so simple,
Yet so sublime-

—Jonathan S. Freeman, ©2011

Part 1
The Landscape of Leadership

*"The Purpose of today's training is to
defeat yesterday's understanding."*

~MIYAMOTO MUSASHI, SIXTEENTH CENTURY SWORDSMAN

Be. Know. Do.

———————————————

The U.S. Military Academy Leadership Manual states that "only by this self-development will you become a confident and competent leader of character." But character and knowledge – while absolutely necessary – are not enough. You cannot be effective, you cannot be a leader, until you *apply* what you know, until you act and *do* what you must. As with skills, you will learn more leadership actions as you serve in different positions. Leadership is about taking action, but there's more to being a leader than what you do. Character and competence – the *be* and the *know* – underlie everything a leader does. So becoming a leader involves developing all aspects of yourself. (Army Leadership "Be, Know, Do" *Leader to Leader.* 26 (Fall 2002): 21-27.)

Although this isn't a book about military leadership, it has benefited from the concepts the military applies, adapts, and views as critical to success. It is about developing wholeness, an integrated approach, and even a definition of *success* that you may not have thought about before as a person who influences others. It will be done simply, with few words, lots of stories and illustrations, and action steps to get moving. As Albert Einstein stated, "Nothing happens until something moves."

Isn't it interesting that the premier command-and-control organization in the world uses "Be. Know. Do." as its credo? If it's fundamental to training the soldiers who often put their lives on the line to serve and protect others, it may prove valuable for the rest of us.

There are no cookie-cutter solutions to leadership challenges, and there are no shortcuts to success. Knowledge is important, but learning is essential. Tools for learning are available to every leader. It is up to you to choose wisely, use them, and work toward mastery in as many areas as you can.

Mastery starts with the "Be." Yet what is *being*? Most of us think that "we are who we are," and "take it or leave it, that's what we have." When was the last time you reflected on who you really are? Not who you *wish* you were, or who you were as a child or teenager, but who you are *now*.

If that one was easy, try asking yourself what you really think about *being*. *What* are you being today? *Who* are you being today? Are you committed to being about something you value, honor, and care about? How do you demonstrate that?

Have you taken a recent inventory of what you know? What you don't know? There are four quadrants of knowledge: 1) what you know you know, 2) what you know you don't know, 3) what you don't know you know, and 4) what you don't know you don't know. Think about that carefully.

Most of the time we focus on the first two; you know about a lot of things, and have confidence that you know them. You also know that you don't know about a lot of things. Hopefully, you have curiosity about some of them and enjoy learning about things you don't know.

This book will focus on the latter two juicy areas: What you don't know you know, either because you have forgotten it or it has become buried as if it is no longer relevant, and those areas about which you don't even know that you don't know; that is, those that require a paradigm shift in order to grasp. These you can relearn or learn anew.

Developing all aspects of ourselves involves both being and knowing. Yet in our culture, the predominant pattern is development of knowledge rather than development of self. I view self-knowledge as the ultimate challenge. The more I think I know, the more I see that I don't know. The more I focus on grabbing and holding on to knowledge, the less valuable it becomes.

As you walk this path, you will see fundamental questions surface again and again. Very little time and attention is paid to the foundations upon which lives are led, how work is performed, and what shapes our organizations. Yet this is exactly what will move us forward to create functional, empowering, and effective places in which to contribute our creative energy. We can grow in a dynamic way – one in which we create ourselves, our organizations, and our world based upon an entirely different view – one based upon the belief that we are not separate from each other, from those we serve, or from the planet. This is the energy of life that beckons us to join in.

What do you know? Do you know what you care about? What don't you know? Are you able to admit when you don't know what you don't know? How are you sure of what you know? Is it because of habit, learned response, or interpretation?

Does what you do reflect what you care about? Does *how you do it* reflect what you care about?

The connection between care and commitment is vital. We act on what we are committed to, and we are committed to what we care about. When you become clear about what you care about, you can engage others in your team and organization in similar discovery. To do this, you must first learn to "be." This simple act will change everything in your world.

Action: Your Care Package

First, center.

Sit in a favorite, quiet spot where you won't be disturbed.

Take a deep, slow inhalation, starting from the belly and breathing through the nose for 7 seconds. Make sure you are breathing from the belly, not from the lungs. The breath from the lungs is shallow and stimulates fear and anxiety; the breath from the belly is from our center, or *dan tien*, and is calming. (*Dan tien* is an Eastern term for the focal point of energy located slightly below the navel, also known as the place of power or the solar plexus.)

Feel the breath as it rises up from the belly all the way to the top of the lungs. Hold the breath for 7 seconds. Then exhale from the top of the lungs all the way back down to your belly as you expel the air through your mouth. Take a full 7 seconds for the exhalation.

Repeat this process 3–5 times. Simply notice what you feel. Pay close attention to the sensations of your experience. This practice is called *centering*, and it is fundamental to all the new work you will be doing.

I invite you to be curious about what you notice when you first begin to center. It may feel awkward at first. In time it will become more comfortable, and likely will become a time that you cherish. From center, true choice is available. Rest in the stillness and power of your center. Feel what you feel. Notice how it is different from the usual frenetic energy of reactivity.

After centering:

1. Take 15 minutes to write in a journal a list of 50 things you care about
*   Then rank, order, and prioritize the top 10
*   Who will you have to *be* in order to accomplish these 10 things?
*   What will you have to *know* in order to accomplish them?
*   What will you have to *do*; what actions will you need to take?

2. Write a list of 10 ways in which you care for yourself. Do it quickly. Write the first 10 things that come to mind. Review the list.

    Is there anything missing that calls for your attention? Where have you put the emphasis in your life? On being? On knowing? On doing? Just notice your priorities. Do you need to allocate your attention differently?

Being is a present-moment exercise. Be committed to it right now, not later. If not now, when?

Make centering a foundational element of your day. Practice it as if your life depends on it.

It will change your world.

The Gift of Change

"As human beings, our greatness lies not so much in being able to remake the world… as in being able to remake ourselves."
—MAHATMA GANDHI

I had the opportunity to visit the southwestern United States, including Arches National Park, Canyon de Chelly National Monument, and Monument Valley Navajo Tribal Park. The latter two are on the Navajo Nation, where native people have lived for centuries. What I experienced there was vastness, beauty, and magnitude unlike anything I had ever seen before. When compared with the sheer brutality of wind and rock, I felt small and insignificant.

Humans have long been dwelling in these areas. Early inhabitants were masters at adaptation. Although the petroglyphs (ancient paintings on rock) show relics of ancestral Pueblo peoples from 500 A.D., there is ample evidence of how these nomadic peoples made the rock, sand, and wind work for them. Native American settlers built upon these foundational dwellings and made them their own. They changed, adapted, and evolved using wisdom traditions that endure to this day. Yet they are in danger of abandoning many of their cultural and language traditions as the younger generation strives to assimilate into modern-day America.

It is this ever-present human ability to live, work, and respond in harmony with nature that beckons. Change is constant, and continuous learning helps us adapt to change. If the native peoples had been resistant to change, they would have perished. Yet change must be managed and directed consciously with regard for what serves and what doesn't serve.

Why are so many in our time resistant to change, when we know that change is the one constant force we can count on in our universe? Any group of people that survived and thrived in challenging circumstances had to learn new ways to adapt, and quickly – learning the new, but not extinguishing the old that deserves preservation.

Learning works both for and against us. Humans are bureaucracies of habits. We lay down habits through our experiences. They are wrapped in thoughts and emotions. Habits, once formed, are like railroad tracks. The trains of our minds run up and down these tracks all day long. This gives us a feeling of predictability and control, yet it is illusory.

These tracks in fact present obstacles to learning new ways. Because we have learned to do and believe many things over the years, they have become ingrained as truths. Although some of the tracks serve us well, many do not. To fulfill our potential, and to help others fulfill theirs, we must be vigilant in examining the "tracks" or habits we have established.

Are you aware that you are always practicing something? Have you given thought to what you practice daily? Which of these do you practice: distraction vs. presence; joy vs. sadness; acceptance vs. judgment; peaceful vs. troubled; anxious vs. calm; satisfied vs. wanting, etc.?

What is so cool about this is that we actually have a *choice* in what we practice. Every moment we *choose* to create more of what we desire or more of what causes suffering. What if you were to cultivate a habit of focusing more on what serves you and less on what you don't want to continue?

To create lasting change in ourselves and in our organizations, the foundation of our *personal bureaucracy* must change, not just our *behaviors*.

The question is: How?

Recent research has shown that the human brain has an extraordinary capacity for neuro-plasticity. That means that new neural pathways are always being created. Isn't that refreshing? Practice, applied consistently over time, creates or reinforces new neural pathways and new habits.

That was the good news. The bad news is that it takes numerous repetitions to create and sustain a new habit. With small steps, practiced consistently over time, the new habits get laid down as new tracks in the brain. They become the new default. With practice it is possible to choose the tracks that guide our thoughts, rather than have our thoughts guided by tracks that no longer serve us.

We think millions of thoughts in a single day. Most of them reinforce our fears. We focus on what we *don't* want, not what we *do* want. If we place attention and energy consciously on what we *do* want, and practice the means to keep our attention focused positively, we allow energy to help us do our work.

What are you waiting for?

Action: *Be a* Change Agent

First, center. As you breathe in slowly and deeply, see in your mind's eye what it is that you want. Move to that space between your eyebrows and hold the image of what you desire. Visualize it. Experience it with all your attention and all your senses. As you breathe, hold your focus there for one minute. If negative thoughts enter, simply notice and release them with ease and grace, returning your focus to what you desire. Breathe deeply into that intention.

When you are relaxed, reflect on the last time you consciously adopted a new habit. Is there something that, if changed, would serve you better?

Afterward in your journal, use these prompts as a challenge to reflect on your patterns around change.

- How will this change work for you?
- What benefits will you or others receive?
- What fears arise when you think of changing?
- What is the cost of not changing this pattern?

What will you consciously focus on creating in the next thirty days? Write it down.

Practice centering daily, at least once.

You'll be amazed at what transpires.

Things are Rarely What They Seem

"We don't see things as they are; we see them as we are."
—ANAIS NIN

Most people see the world as they *think* it is, not as a reflection of how they *are*. How many realize that our external realities are projections of our inner states of mind? When faced with a big decision, a challenge, a difficult conversation, a job change, or any number of common problems, people often struggle with what to *do* rather than how they *see*.

In my experience as a coach, problems and concerns are almost never about what to *do*, but rather about how we see and who we *are*. *Who we are being* allows us to bring our most precious resources to any situation.

Let's look at an example from history. Although hand washing is now a rigorously mandated policy in hospitals, in the mid-1800s the idea of germs being spread via touching had not yet surfaced. Doctors would go from touching dead, infected bodies to touching mothers giving birth without first cleaning their hands. Consequently, according to the National Health Museum, 25 percent of women who delivered their babies in hospitals died from infections. Dr. Ignaz Semmelweis observed the alarming death rate and suggested that deaths might decrease if doctors washed their hands more. Semmelweis was ridiculed, and later suffered a mental breakdown.

We now know that the way people thought about the problem limited their ability to actually see new solutions. They did what they had always done out of habit, not realizing that the answer was in the way they were *thinking* about the problem. They didn't know what they didn't know. When that changed, the solution was apparent. This is an example of a paradigm shift.

What paradigms predominate in life for you? Do you think about the possibility that what may seem to be fact is really just an incomplete set of beliefs that you can alter or expand?

Neuroscience research has shown that over 90 percent of human thought is automatic and comes from the subconscious mind. It is based on our primitive fears. Humans are hard-wired for fear based on our evolutionary need to survive as a species. Our hard-wired fear actually helped keep us alive in earlier times.

Yet how does that wiring impact us in today's world? Although for most people there is little likelihood of being eaten by a bear, we often act *as if* we are in that predicament. We see and experience stressors all day long, and respond habitually through our reactive, fear-based state. How many times has it happened that we hear something that is concerning or unsettling, and immediately respond as if an imaginary bear were attacking us? This is because the brain's emotional centers can't distinguish between the real and the imaginary.

When a scary experience presents itself, the amygdala gets hijacked. This part of the brain stores and processes emotional reactions. Once activated, the "fight or flight" mechanism kicks in. Cortisol and adrenaline pump out like crazy to help in the flight from the imaginary bear. The problem is, there *is* no bear. Our response is due to emotional wiring that was programmed from our experience to respond as if there really was a bear.

If over 90 percent of human thought is automatic, that leaves less than 10 percent that is conscious. Think about that for a minute. What if that could be expanded even to 20 percent? What if it were possible to double the number of conscious thoughts? What if that number were tripled or quadrupled? What if many more people were to expand conscious thought? What if there was learning and practice that helped develop this? How would that impact our work and relationships?

Consider how our world would be different if we spent more energy on increasing conscious thought rather than subjecting ourselves to the dictates of the habit-seeking subconscious. Pondering such a thought is something for which I am willing to stay up late!

Action : **Beliefs are a Powerful Thing**

1. Make a list of three beliefs about a challenge you are having. Underneath each one provide evidence – that is, factual proof – that those beliefs are irrefutably true. Now write what you can do about it given those beliefs are true.

2. Next write a "New Belief" column. Underneath each of the three beliefs write three different assumptions that *could* be true. What actions and outcomes would be possible if those different assumptions informed your beliefs and actions?

As a special free reader bonus, I have prepared a Step Up Leader Action Guide to accompany this book. It will assist you in getting the most out of the exercises. To obtain it, simply visit www.StepUpLeader.com and click on "Action Guide."

The Dream in the Maze

The other day I realized
That this is just a maze,
Where our own thoughts create the walls
Obscured in ancient haze.

And soon I came to understand
That we too have a guide;
A dwindling Fire fueled by dream
That hungers deep inside.

Yet rather than give heed to that
Which we necessitate,
We climb a billion concrete walls
In semi-lucid state.

Thus dimmer still becomes the Light
That yearns to lead us through
And soon that Flame ebbs out of sight,
Forsaking me and you.

—JONATHAN S. FREEMAN, © 2011

Part II
Break it Down

—◆—

"It takes a lot of courage to release the familiar and seemingly secure, to embrace the new. But there is no real security in what is no longer meaningful. There is more security in the adventurous and exciting, for in movement there is life, and in change there is power."

‑Alan Cohen

Underlying Conversations

"Our fate is shaped from within ourselves outward, never from without inward."
—Jacques Lasseyran

One of the most amazing moments of learning for me happened when I came to experience and understand the power of an "underlying conversation." An underlying conversation is a belief structure or mindset that precedes thought and, ultimately, behavior. The human mind accumulates knowledge through observation, action, and repetition. Out of these experiences interpretations are made that may or may not have validity. These interpretations can render us ineffective or be quite harmful. When they are repeated often enough, they morph into "truth" and are expressed as "the way things are."

Upon closer examination, these so-called truths (really fabrications) control our actions. They begin as small threads spun from experiences, and gradually, with repetition, evolve into larger threads. Over many years, they grow into fabric that is strong and resistant, exerting an influence on our beliefs and approaches, and limiting the actions we see as possible.

Rest assured that *everyone* has these fabrications. It is impossible to be human and *not* have them. Although we actually have lots of them, there is usually one major one that supersedes the others. When it is revealed, a lot of high-priced real estate in the brain is available for more productive investments.

The cost of *not* discovering an underlying conversation is big. Consider Yvette, for whom this exploration radically changed her ability to reach her professional and personal goals. When she discovered her underlying conversation, she saw the common thread that led her to poor food choices, lack of focus, and avoidance of task completion.

She appreciated that it wasn't *really* her (at least not consciously). There was another part of her, of which she had no conscious awareness, that had taken control. She explored this "controller," remembering that she had grown up in a large family in which she had flown under the radar. Although this style helped her in her position as one of the younger siblings, her *interpretation* throughout childhood was that she didn't matter because she didn't count. This belief led to a host of behaviors, including avoidance. She acted in a manner consistent with the belief that she *didn't* count. In doing so, she reinforced the earlier established patterns and created circumstances that strengthened the patterning. She got to be *right* instead of *happy.*

When she avoided, she relinquished her power. That made her feel invisible, which in turn, made her feel safe. This was a huge obstacle in her life. It caused her to be disappointed, shameful, and embarrassed because she did not follow through on things. This influenced her choices across the board.

Once she was able to see this consistent, repetitive pattern for what it truly was, she was able to shift *out of it.* The result was that she accomplished her goals, including improved focus, better self-care, and more energy, as well as better accountability and execution. Through her own experience, she became a better listener.

Julie had an underlying conversation about perfection. For recovering perfectionists, there is almost always a sub-current of guilt. They never feel as if they are doing enough, or doing enough well. Underneath her operating system was a program about her mother, who felt guilty about working too much. She had subconsciously adopted this conversation during childhood as if it were her own. As an adult, this software continued to run in the background, courtesy of the powerful subconscious mind. The trouble for her was that it was unseen and un-acknowledged. Therefore it had power over her. A lot of power.

Julie had a breakthrough moment when she realized she had unknowingly adopted her mother's patterns and was living as if they were her own. This affected her at work and at home. She created a hectic work environment that sabotaged her capacity for success and balance. Simply by uncovering the underlying conversation, it no longer "ran" her.

Underlying conversations are influenced by a person's group or "tribal" influence. These cultural factors shape people in subtle, yet potent ways. They include familial, geographic, national, religious, gender, and racial forces. Cultural influences are a potent presence in underlying conversations, and should always be examined.

A professional coaching relationship offers a vehicle for safely exploring an underlying conversation without diving into the realm of therapy. Coaching aims to reveal how a particular underlying conversation may be affecting a person's ability to reach their goals. Underlying conversations are small structures built around our fears. Then the subconscious mind reinforces these structures through repetition. The good news is that while it may take a long time to build them up, they can be torn down in one moment.

We grow a great deal when we get a handle on what underlying conversation is operating in the background of our brain's subconscious. It is often an outmoded program that runs the mainframe of our busy lives. That is the bad news. The good news is that we have the capacity to install new software and run different programs.

Explore:

- What operating system are you running? Have you consciously chosen it? If so, what process helped you discover it? With what did you replace it?

- What cultural forces influence you? How many can you identify? What stories do you believe based on those forces that shape your current decisions?

- What operating systems are running your team? How do you know? What evidence do you have? Are they serving the team goals or sabotaging them?

- What about your team and those with whom you work? Are you aware of their cultural influences? Are they? How does this impact how they behave and perform?

Action : **What software is running?**

The next time you are in a conversation with a colleague, friend, or family member, ask yourself, "What operating system might be operating in this person?" Then ask a question that might help that person uncover it.

Make sure you do this in a spirit of genuine curiosity rather than judgment.

We can never discern someone else's underlying conversation. We can only observe when they discover it for themselves.

Sick and Tired

———◆———

"In order to change, we must be sick and tired of being sick and tired."
—AUTHOR UNKNOWN

The typical course of action taken when we don't get what we want is to change the action. Trial and error. Keep trying different things until something happens that is satisfactory. Most people expect that by taking new actions, different results should be produced. Why is this often not the case?

Because the *person* producing the actions hasn't changed. If the person can't or won't consider how the problem is viewed, there isn't a chance to *see new possibilities*. In fact, most of the breakthrough opportunities lie far beyond what is often seen on the first pass or through instinct. When someone finally becomes sick and tired, it is often the first time they can glimpse into the future they desire.

We prefer *homeostasis*, a Greek word meaning "similar" or "standing still." It means a system that regulates its internal environment by maintaining a stable, constant condition. Because of this innate tendency, human growth rarely comes about when things are going well. We usually grow when the great two-by-fours of life strike. There is little incentive and lots of inertia for preventing anything from happening until sick-and-tired forces change upon us.

Sick-and-tired can be figurative, as well as literal. When figurative, a person says, "I am sick and tired of the way this isn't working," or "I am sick and tired of the way this team never meets deadlines," or "I am sick and tired of how my boss manages this project." Sick-and-tired is the operative moment; it causes a person to poke their head up out of the proverbial muck and pronounce, "I am ready for something different. I don't know what that is, but I do know that I am not going to continue doing *this* any longer."

In organizations, people typically develop work-arounds. When a system becomes unworkable, and the people in it become sick and tired of how things take place, they often develop compensatory mechanisms to address the problem. Only when these mechanisms show up as repeated failures do organizational systems ask for help. (Sometimes long after!) By the time help does show up, there is often a lot of collateral damage. The compensatory systems are not only dysfunctional, but also deeply entrenched.

On an individual level, sick-and-tired can show up literally in our bodies. Why? Because what goes on in the mind is continuously fed to every cell of the body. Cells and organs receive these signals as if they are radio frequencies. Strong, positive signals equal strong, healthy, functional cells. The opposite is also true; weakened, distressed, and erratic signals produce malfunction and sickness.

This is not the human birthright. People were designed to be healthy, well, functional, energetic beings. Do most people fit this description? Do you? Look at the people around you. What do you observe in them? How are they caring for their bodies and minds? The outer is a reflection of the inner. What are they reflecting? Can you inspire others by taking action for yourself?

Jim was the founder of a successful business in the health care industry. He worked hard in a focused way and built a reputable business with a small team. As the business grew, so did his troubles. He had to manage others *and* take care of himself.

He wanted to work on growing his business and meeting hefty, expanding goals. He was open to changing and growing, as were most of his team. What he didn't expect was the toll that the constant stress, pressure, and worry had taken on his physical body.

Not long into our work together, Jim developed some shortness of breath. He went through a full cardiac workup, and fortunately everything checked out. But he had been given an early warning sign.

As a result of our work together, Jim learned how to alleviate pressure and stress. He developed skills to increase conversational effectiveness, accountability, and trust. He also learned about the power of breath and centering. This gave him more control and choice, and alleviated reactivity and the resulting stress. The stage had been set for Jim's business to thrive and sustain the growth. His health improved, and he now has tools that he can use in the future.

Just as we make deposits and earn interest on our money in bank accounts, so do we make deposits and withdrawals in our health accounts. An extended period of time in which we withdraw and don't deposit will leave a negative balance, both in the bank and in the body.

If you are feeling poorly, take a good hard look at the state of your "health account."

If you feel terrific, I acknowledge you for understanding and living in harmony with your body and its needs.

Action: Sick and Tired

1. Take your own Sick-and-Tired Inventory. What is it that you are sick and tired of in the world of work? Make a list of 5 things.
   - Which are within your control to act upon?
   - What have you done about them?
   - What possibilities do you see for doing things differently now?

   Next examine your own health and well-being. How well do you care for yourself? Do you engage in practices that support a well-functioning body and mind? Without the two, you are leaving lots of capacity on the table (likely on the doctor's table).

2. Make a list of 5 things about your body and how it feels that you are sick and tired about. Consider the following prompts for your journal:
   - What is one thing you do that you know doesn't help your body but you do it anyway?
   - What belief do you think would have to change for you to eliminate that one thing?
   - What would it take to do that?
   - What would the payoff be of doing so?

Be at Peace, Not War

"*You can't shake hands with a clenched fist.*"
—INDIRA GANDHI

I see this as one of the biggest issues faced in homes, communities, organizations, states, and beyond. People are at war, and it isn't just about military force or weaponry.

We are at war when we are disconnected from the value others bring to the conversation – when we argue and defend a position because we have to be right. We are at war when we cut in line in traffic, when we grab for internal resources at the expense of our colleagues, and when we engage in practices that undermine structures intended for the safety and welfare of customers. The results of being at war are everywhere.

Being at war is symptomatic of a deeper problem. It is a reflection of our being at war with ourselves.

The best model I have encountered on this topic comes from *The Anatomy of Peace: Resolving the Heart of Conflict* published by the Arbinger Institute in 2006. The work outlined in this book forms the basis for understanding the root cause of conflict. The model is based on the notion of "collusion." The reasoning goes: "When I betray myself, I become self-deceived. Then I inflate others' faults. As a result, I inflate my own virtue. Then I inflate the value of things that justify my self-betrayal. In the end I blame the other." We provoke each other to do more of what we say we don't like about the other. The book defines this entire process as "being in the box."

"We put ourselves in boxes, and then we put others in boxes. We live insanely when we're in the box, desperate to show that we're justified. When we're feeling overwhelmed, it generally isn't our obligation to others, but our in-the-box desperation to prove something about ourselves that we find overwhelming." (*Leadership and Self-Deception,* The Arbinger Institute, 2006.)

James had a habit of labeling David, his co-worker, as lazy. When we began working together, the relationship between the two men had eroded, so much so that having productive conversations wasn't possible. Self-esteem suffered for both of them. After an intervention in which they began to break down the barriers to honest, trusting communication, this changed. As the boxes came down, David's effectiveness in his role improved. The two men actually grew to become respectful, trusted colleagues, and were able to go after more important things than each other.

Parents of teenagers may find the following to be familiar: Valerie labels her son Justin as lazy, irresponsible, and self-absorbed. He withdraws, and is careless and scattered in doing his chores. Valerie sees this behavior and reacts by complaining, criticizing, and dispensing consequences. What Justin sees is an unloving, critical, and dictatorial parent. Distance between them grows unbearable. Sound familiar?

In this scenario, everything Valerie does when in her box actually provokes Justin to be the opposite of what she desires. The very behavior she complains about is behavior that then justifies her actions. In the box, there is mutual mistreatment and mutual justification.

By being in a box ourselves, we provoke or reinforce problems in others.

What is the key to getting out of the box? Slow down and *care.* Our boxes are penetrated by the humanity of others. Learn to honor others as people.

The moment this occurs, they become real people with needs, hopes, and worries that are as legitimate as our own. When this happens, you are out of the box!

In what ways are you, your team, or your organization at war internally and externally? Who in your organization have you kept in a box?

Bringing peace into our world begins with every single one of us. Redirecting energy with an eye toward getting out of the box is a powerful way to joyfully influence others.

Commit to leading and inspiring others on a peaceful path.

Action : **Unwrapping the Box**

First, center. Then reflect while journaling on the following:

1. What boxes am I in, and in what boxes do I place others?

2. Draw a sample box for a situation at work that is challenging.
    - How are you in the box?
    - How do others respond that keeps them in their box and you in your box?
    - What will you need to do to get out of the box?
    - What will it take to do it?
    - How will you know when you have been successful?
    - How will others respond when you view them as people and show empathy for their needs and goals?
    - How is that different from what you experience now?

3. Make a list of ways in which you could get out of the box.
    - Which ones will you choose to act on?
    - What will the payoff be?

The Power of Stopping

"To win, you must be present."
—SIGN ABOVE A BINGO PARLOR DOOR

We are a society in constant motion. Most of us run around till we are exhausted and lifeless. Stopping means falling asleep.

The truth is that most people are already asleep – asleep in life, sleepwalking with habits, self-programmed with actions and repetitive behaviors. We may never stop to consider whether this is working for us.

Asking this question sent me on a journey of three thousand miles. I had an epiphany at a Zen Silent Meditation Retreat on the Pacific Ocean. I flew across the United States to learn that everything I thought I knew needed to be forgotten. I had gone to California seeking lessons and teachers, but what I didn't expect was that they would be in the form of rocks.

I had signed up for complete silence for the entire five days. We were forbidden to use phones, radios, portable electronics, or books – no distractions. There was nothing to do but deal with the chattering of my Western "monkey-mind." Mine had been wandering aimlessly for two solid days. Sometimes the thoughts were about comfort, boredom, frustration, or hunger. Then they turned to: "What am I doing here?" "I don't get it." "What is there to get?" "What if I am not getting anything?" "I will have flown across the United States to sit in silence and not get what I came here for."

Miraculously, on the third day, my mind settled down and the more prevalent thought became: "Whatever I get will be exactly what I need, and it will be perfect."

I had been practicing the Zen dictum: "Look, See, Rest, Let Be." In one of the practice sessions during a guided meditation, a strong thump and pull in my gut occurred. It got stronger and stronger. I knew it was a sign to pay attention. Eventually it became so distracting that I decided to leave the room and go outside for a walk.

Making my way toward the ocean, I walked in silence alone for over a mile or so. I let myself get carried away by the crashing waves breaking on the enormous rocks in the distance. I came upon a beautiful alcove and decided to sit and rest. My eyes gazed upon a collection of large rocks in the distance. I watched as the large Pacific waves crashed against these rocks, causing fountains of ocean spray to scatter with loud, thundering peals.

I had been there for a while, just soaking up the sounds and visuals of a magnificent landscape I rarely got to see – sitting in silence, watching and waiting – and after twenty minutes or so, the rocks began to move. I blinked in disbelief. How could these enormous immovable structures move? Yet they had.

What occurred to me after a few moments was that a family of sea lions had been relaxing on the rocks. After a lengthy and satisfying rest, they began to stretch and play. Because nature had designed them to be so well camouflaged on the rocks, they truly appeared to *be* rocks. That is, until they moved.

They had become one with the structures beneath them. Had I been in a hurry, or on auto-pilot in a power-walk, or distracted, I would have missed this Moment of The Moving Rocks.

Yet isn't that what people do a lot? Don't they rush through the moments of life, often missing the miracles that unfold? The sea lions taught me the lesson I had gone there to learn. For me, the sea lions represented the magnificence that happens in every moment when time stops and true presence is our experience.

What and who might the sea lions be in your life?

This simple question has the power to change your life. In order to influence others, you simply must be present. Without presence there is only automatic, reflexive thought and action. New possibilities are unlikely to emerge. To create, there must be presence. To relate, there must be presence. To care, there must be presence.

So it follows that "presence" is a gift to open right NOW.

Action : **Developing Presence**

1. Commit to an exercise of stopping for just a few moments several times a day. Sit or stand tall. Take several deep breaths and close your eyes. Try focusing on your senses other than sight.
   - What do you hear when you stop?
   - What do you smell when you stop?
   - What do you feel when you stop?
   - What sensations do you notice in your body?

   Just simply notice and create awareness of the benefit of stopping, even if just for three minutes at first.

2. Then challenge yourself to longer and more frequent "stopping moments."
   - What were you able to observe during these longer periods?
   - Write in your journal about what you noticed and experienced.

What did this exercise reveal that you may have been missing?

Did the sea lions in your life move?

Silence is Golden

"Hello darkness, my old friend
I've come to talk with you again
Because a vision softly creeping
Left its seeds while I was sleeping
And the vision that was planted in my brain
Still remains
Within the sound of silence"
—Paul Simon, *The Sound of Silence*

As with many sayings, the origin of the phrase "Silence is golden" is obscure. There are reports of versions dating back to ancient Egypt. The first example in English is from the poet Thomas Carlyle, who translated the phrase from German in 1831 in *Sartor Resartus*, in which a character expounds at length on the virtues of silence:

"Silence is the element in which great things fashion themselves together; that at length they may emerge, fully-formed and majestic, into the daylight of Life, which they are thenceforth to rule. Speech too is great, but not the greatest... As the Swiss Inscription says: Sprecfien ist silbern, Schweigen ist golden (Speech is silver, Silence is golden); or as I might rather express it: Speech is of Time, Silence is of Eternity."

If silence is indeed "of eternity," why do most of us spend so little time there? Have you ever noticed how we fill our airwaves with constant soundtracks? It is impossible to go into a public area today without hearing radio or television in an office, elevator, restaurant, or airport, and sometimes we hear sounds from both radio and television at the same time!

We get in our cars and turn on cell phones or radios to listen to news (other people talking) or music (other people singing). Rarely do we simply listen to our own breath. We hardly ever notice our own moods, emotions, or even our own thoughts; how could we possibly notice those of other people? We allow our internal experience, thoughts, and emotions to be controlled by external sounds, rather than experiencing our true internal state of silence and presence.

During my Zen Silent Meditation Retreat, there was complete silence. There was only silence, every day, all day, even at meals. You may think this would be impossible. (My family sure did!) Eventually my discomfort with silence ceded to enjoyment. I began to notice the subtle flavors of food and tried to identify the spices. I also became acutely aware of the quantity of food I ate. As I chewed each bite slowly, carefully, and without talking, I actually became full with less. What a metaphor for life.

Ask yourself if you are uncomfortable with silence. I was. People often try to fill in gaps in conversations, as if there is something wrong with a pause or quiet.

When I began professionally coaching others, silence made me uncomfortable. It left a gap in the conversation that felt awkward at first. I tried to fill in the spaces when there was silence. But soon I learned to trust that silence is often the greatest teacher. It allows connection with the deep knowing that is always there but that we rarely experience. Without silence, we live in a repetitive, habitual state. With it, there is a chance for magnificence.

How are you avoiding silence in your life? What might be the price you pay for this? How might this impact your ability to influence others?

Silence is an opportunity to notice and experience yourself and others differently.

Play with silence. Try it. See what unfolds. It will work its magic for you.

Action: **Silence is Golden**

Create a new practice of cultivating silence in your life, and see what happens.

This could involve making a commitment to take one daily car or walking trip without music or radio, or eating a meal with another in silence. Challenge yourself with being silent when you will be sure to notice the impact.

It is possible that in silence you, too, may find gold.

Curious George Had It Right

"I have no particular talent. I am merely passionately curious."
—ALBERT EINSTEIN

How many people are learners? The modern, technological world requires people to continually learn new things. But does that imply that we are truly learners, or simply that we are obsessed with acquiring new knowledge with which to act? Learning is about *far* more than acquiring knowledge or tools.

Learning is a mindset. As human beings, we share the fact that "enemies of learning" operate under the radar in our powerful, subconscious minds. The enemies include:

- Being unable to admit "I don't know"
- Not knowing that you don't know, but acting as if you do
- Being unaware that we live in blindness
- Being arrogant
- Using lack of time as an excuse, or not taking the time
- Gravity – taking things too seriously
- Triviality – not taking things seriously enough
- Confusing your opinions with knowledge
- Believing that learning equals gathering information

- Wanting to be right about everything all the time
- Being addicted to answers
- Not including emotions as a domain of learning
- Not including the body as a domain of learning
- Analyzing to the point of paralysis

Learners engage the world in a spirit of curiosity. This is antithetical to knowing and judging, which happens when people believe they already *know* what is best or right. By contrast, when someone approaches a conversation or problem from a place of genuine curiosity, there is space for the other to self-express.

The greatest discoveries in science come from curiosity. A fundamental question is asked, an elemental truth is revealed, which leads to another question, and then another and another. Ultimately there is penetration of an idea at a truly deep level. A scientist never knows where a question will lead. They only know to keep *asking*. That is how Einstein discovered the Theory of Relativity. It is also the path of many Nobel Prize winners.

Are you focused on asking questions? Do you listen for what unfolds?

What I have learned from coaching is that very few of us have developed a talent and passion for questions. We have been educated and reinforced systematically to have answers. We have been rewarded for being right, and not for being curious. We are addicted to answers.

How would your world be different if you lived and acted as a learner and not a knower? How would this impact the capacities of others? Your team? Your organization?

What are the most common enemies lurking in your learning?

By simply being curious, much learning and wisdom can unfold. I have been amazed at what happens when I ask people to "tell me a story about a time when…". Then I follow up with "How does that relate to the situation you are in today?"

Almost always the answers reveal truths that help them with their current situation or problem.

Curiosity requires getting out of the left brain and into the right brain. The left brain is ruled by logic and rationality. It doesn't naturally gravitate toward the synthetic, integrative energy of curiosity. To fuel curiosity, you can practice accessing the right hemisphere of creativity more often.

It is a skill worth developing.

Action : Behind Enemy Lines: Curiosity

1. Spend five minutes with a friend or family member telling a story about one of the listed "enemies of learning" and its impact on your ability to solve a problem. Then switch and listen to your friend do the same. Start with the most commonly encountered enemy and eventually work through the others in a similar fashion.

    Paying attention to how this bias operates yields profound shifts just by itself.

2. Make a practice of spending a day asking questions from a place of genuine curiosity. What did you notice about the type of conversations you had?
    *   How were they different?
    *   How did your outcomes change?
    *   How did your relationships change?
    *   Did you see any new possibilities that weren't available to you before?

3. You may do the following standing or sitting: Cross your right elbow to your left knee and vice versa for 10-12 counts. Do four sets of repetitions. This helps to energetically synchronize the right and left hemispheres across the *corpus collosum*. By accessing the whole brain more often, you will enable new neural pathways to crossover, thereby utilizing more of your whole brain. Curiosity will follow.

    With practice, curiosity will become part of your everyday capability.

Questions versus Answers

We live in an answer-directed society. From the earliest age in school, students are taught that they need to have answers. The person with the most right answers gets the highest score on a test. We are also taught that mastery of material comes from having answers. We are rarely rewarded for asking questions.

But what if the questions are really where the action is? How often are you rewarded for asking questions? What would happen if our conversations consisted of more questions than answers?

This orientation toward answers derives from the predominant ego-oriented thinking that has existed and strengthened throughout the centuries. The ego needs to evaluate, assess, judge, and criticize. It separates us from others. We listen to answers that agree with our preconceived thinking; those that vary from it get discarded as nonsense. Often, in the process of dismissing the answers, we dismiss the person as well.

I see this as a major problem in the world today. There are many people with answers but very few people asking questions. And when questions are asked, they often don't seem like the right ones, and come from a presumption that there are right and a wrong answers rather than from a genuine interest in what others have to say.

Effective questions promote discovery and learning. They invoke the whole brain, including the rational, logical, concrete skills of the left hemisphere and the synthetic, creative, integrative skills of the right hemisphere.

Asking questions also helps speakers hear the answers for themselves. In speaking, a person can clarify something they may not have truly understood before then. At the end of the day, what is communicated through asking questions versus stating answers is "I accept you." When these kinds of questions are asked, it sends an acceptance message to the responder, who then responds more positively. This generative cycle of acceptance feeds on itself.

"What" and "how" questions are more effective than "why" questions, particularly if they focus on open-ended possibilities. These types of questions allow a person to craft a thoughtful and often creative response, rather than a defensive one.

For example, have you noticed that when someone asks a lot of questions it can feel as if you are being interrogated? Sometimes you just shut down because you feel invaded. Questions asked in this manner often don't seem to come from genuine curiosity. It feels more like control.

Another important element in asking effective questions is to frame them in a way that will move someone *toward* what they desire and *away* from the current way of looking at the problem. The more the person focuses on what isn't working, the more they become stuck in repetitive thought. When they are heard by a listener with an open ear toward a different result in the future, there are new possibilities. When those possibilities are spoken, the person declares a new future and literally speaks it into existence.

I have learned that there is no perfect question and no list of great questions. A question is only as good as its context. The right question at the wrong time is the wrong question. However, a good question is made more powerful by the spirit in which it is spoken. Many times when I had no questions whatsoever, a question popped into my head that cracked open a thorny issue. I learned that when I open myself to what may unfold, I allow that possibility to unfold for others.

I try to avoid advising and answering questions for people I am coaching. My human tendency wanders toward the ego-dominated "I know what to do about this." However, it is not *my* knowing that has any relevance. The critical answers are revealed in the *questions* I may be privileged enough to formulate. Only then can a person make a new declaration and speak it into existence.

The art of questioning may be one of the most important qualities to develop for people who influence others. Get committed to examining the quality of your questions and watch what unfolds.

Action: Questions, Questions and More Questions

First, center.

1. Prepare your journal and reflect on the following over the course of a week:
    *   Do you offer more answers than questions in a day?
    *   How does this impact others?

2. Try conducting a conversation without presenting answers. Only ask questions, and be prepared to listen intently to the responses.
    *   What unfolds?
    *   How is this a different game?
    *   What is the value of this to you and to others?

Listening Isn't Hearing

"I want to do for you what the spring does for the cherry trees."
—PABLO NERUDA

How many people know how to listen? Sure, there is listening to the hum-drum sounds and signals from computers, cell phones, ambulances, radios, iPods, etc. But do we listen to other people?

How much is actually being heard? Is the focus on anticipating what someone is going to say or on finishing their sentences? Are we thinking about what might happen next or about what happened yesterday? Are we thinking about everything *but* what the speaker is trying to communicate?

What I have learned through coaching is that one of the most powerful acts in which I can participate as a human being is to *hear* another. When I listen with *all* of me, fully present only in that moment, something magical happens. It is not me and my thoughts that inhabit the space; it is the speaker and the listener, having an exchange, speaking and witnessing.

In those moments, a new world is created. When I truly listen, I become more of who *I* am. Hopefully the speaker can say the same.

Listening involves attending to more than words; it also involves per-ception of the tone of voice and body language. How often have you had someone tell you that you were attacking them when your words were simple, direct, and lacking accusation? Likely they were responding not to the words, but to the tone and pitch of your voice. Learning to attend to and control this element of communication is just as important as the actual spoken word, because it influences how the listener *hears*.

Amanda had a strong set of beliefs that she thought were true. However, in a coaching conversation, she discovered that she was actually imagining they were true, and running her life as if they were. She found that the barriers she experienced were a wall that she could break through with a few powerful words. Until she spoke about her beliefs and was *heard* and witnessed, she did not appreciate how much the imaginary had influenced and therefore limited her.

Paulette changed the negatively charged dynamic with her boss because she learned to listen differently. Richard was able to turn around a difficult relationship with a team member by learning to listen differently. Lorraine was fearful of making a big career move and hadn't thought about what was really stopping her from taking action. When she finally spoke about what was stopping her, and was truly heard, the grip of fear that had previously paralyzed her released its hold. The result was that she created a job description for her life after a long period of indecision and stalling. She took action to move ahead with a job change.

Consider ways in which you can shift the quality of your listening. For example, commit to having communication when you can make direct eye contact with the other person. If you or the other persons is unable to do this, re-schedule for a better time to have the conversation. Commit to abstinence from computer screens and cell phones when speaking or listening. Other people may not see that you are distracted by these things, but they certainly feel it.

If you find yourself unable to listen intently, take one or two very slow and deep inhalations, make eye contact with the other, and tell yourself, "Be here now. This moment will never come again. Will I regret missing it?"

It can be interesting to practice listening from the perspective of "what is the story that is *not* being spoken about here?" Sometimes the act of listening carefully and asking a question that is simple and direct can help the speaker uncover a pattern of observing and acting.

What is it that you do as a listener? What are your patterns? What do you want to improve? How will you do that? How will that serve you?

The art of listening is one of the most important qualities to develop for people who influence others. Examine the quality of your listening and hearing. Tune in to what changes around you. Revel in your discovery.

Action : **What Did You Say?**

1. First, assess what kind of listener you are. Is it different in each relationship? What is the quality of your listening in respect to your partner, your children, your parents, your team, your boss, your colleagues?

    Are you:

    *   Fully committed?
    *   Distracted – with attention fading in and out?
    *   Anxious – listening and interrupting so you don't forget what you want to say?
    *   Inattentive – looking everywhere *but* at the speaker?
    *   Impatient – "Hurry up; I've got somewhere to go."?

2. Practice today paying full attention to *one* person in *one* conversation. Stay fully present with them, as if this were the only and *most* important conversation of your life. As if everything that happened in that conversation really mattered to you.

    *   How did that feel different than your usual? How did that person react? What was the outcome?
    *   How would you be able to change your relationship to that individual by listening like this again?
    *   What kind of feedback did you receive?

Conversational Architecture

"Your word is the power that you have to create.
Through the word you express your creative power.
Regardless of what language you speak, your intent manifests
through the word.
The word is a force.
It is the power you have to create the events in your life."
—Don Miguel Ruiz, *The Four Agreements*

People often pay more attention to the structure of the buildings around them and those they inhabit than they do to their conversations. Sometimes they come away from a conversation unsure about what just happened or what they are going to do next. There may be confusion as to whether there was an agreement or not. There may be an unresolved issue or an imagined promise. The worst-case scenario is when there is no clarity. The result is often that trust is damaged and neither party knows how it happened. After all, they did have a conversation.

My experience in coaching people reveals that this problem is widespread. I suppose it is because most people have never learned about the anatomy of a conversation. They don't know how language can be used not just to *describe*, but to *create* a desired future.

People often believe that because they are well-spoken and articulate, they are good communicators. What they often don't realize is that communication is about *way* more than words. It is important to understand the structure of language and the way we use speech to create our world. This includes discerning what conversation we are actually *in*.

The distinction between a conversation *for action* and a conversation *for possibility* is crucial. A lack of clarity as to the *nature* of the conversation can cause confusion and a poor outcome. Conversely, setting an intention and declaring what conversation we are having sets the stage for a successful outcome. Most people mix them up; they begin in one conversation and often end up in another.

Conversations for action are intended to move an idea, project, or action item forward. As a result, something tangible will be accomplished. There is an agreed-upon desire for a specific outcome.

Conversations for possibility are those in which the participants envision, brainstorm, and co-create. Conversations for possibility do not necessarily elicit a direct outcome in that particular moment. Outcomes may ensue in the future, but this specific conversation is for exchanging ideas, values, and cares. Out of such a conversation there may emerge subsequent conversations in which there is a directed purpose of action.

Pay attention to the missing conversations at work and in your personal life. What conversations do you need to have that you haven't had? What conversations do you feel you cannot have? What conversations, if you had them, would enable something important to happen that needs to happen? What conversations have you had that went poorly? How could you re-do them differently? What would it take to do so?

Another important component of conversational architecture is a request. Most people assume that when they speak, the listener hears their requests without the speaker actually having to ask for something. This is usually not the case. A request requires six elements: a committed speaker, a committed listener, a future action with conditions of satisfaction, a timeframe, a mood, and context (showing how the request fits into a bigger picture). When any of these elements is lacking, there is usually a communication breakdown.

People often find that when they reflect on why there is an intractable problem, it can be traced back to conversational anatomy. Simple awareness of what was actually said, heard, and understood leads to change. *Mastering* the art of conversational architecture allows for profound and lasting shifts in relationships, influence, and accountability.

Once the building blocks of conversational architecture are at your disposal, you have the power to see those elements in which you are proficient, and those you need to develop. For example, people who become frustrated and easily stressed often have difficulty making requests for help. They assume that others see how much they have going on, expecting them to offer help. When help doesn't arrive, they can become frustrated, resentful, and angry.

Conversational architecture was the framework that helped Sue identify and conquer her long-standing pattern of being overwhelmed. Her tendency to become frustrated and resentful was exacerbated because she didn't ask for help. Once she learned about requests, she was able to use language to eliminate the patterns that triggered her emotional default of frustration and anger – so simple, yet very effective.

Organizations are complex networks of conversation. When conversations are ineffective or non-existent, productivity and trust break down. Without strong conversational muscle, people are often not speaking and listening in the same language. It may be in English, but the misunderstandings are there just the same.

When people learn how to make an effective request, they can prevent emotions from being a first line of defense. They have more control, stability, and calm in the face of challenging circumstances. When you learn how to get a promise, you have something you can manage, and you have a way to track accountability.

What have you done to develop yourself in the art of conversational anatomy?

Action : **Building Blocks of Conversation**

1. Pay attention to whether you are feeling harmonious in your relationships at work and at home. Are you resentful? Do you feel resigned in some area? If so, conversational anatomy is probably playing a role.

   Think about a recent conversation. What agreement did you get? Were you able to make a request? What did you do when the promise was broken?

2. Explore the common patterns in your communication breakdown by making a list of several examples and looking for commonality.

3. Are there specific conversations that you haven't had and need to have?
   • What are they and with whom?
   • When will you commit to having them?
   • What will be the payoff?

The Landscape of Moods and Emotions Isn't a Still Life

"People who lean on logic and philosophy and rational exposition end by starving the best part of the mind."
—William Butler Yeats

How many people walk around in unhappy states that don't serve them or others? The following are commonly heard complaints:

"I'm just in a bad mood."
"What she said made me sad."
"Nothing I do anymore seems right."

As human beings, we are motivated and influenced by moods and emotions far more often than we care to admit. The subconscious mind stores both memories of events *and* the associated emotions. A memory gets triggered by what we perceive as a similar circumstance, bringing with it the associated emotion, and we often react in ways that are unfitting or even inappropriate to the circumstance at hand. This can cause subsequent emotions to arise, including confusion, frustration, anger, and shame.

The underlying assumption is that this is out of our control. We believe that somehow we got *into* this state and somehow we will get *out* of it. People often hope for an external stimulus to make them feel better. They may not believe that there will be an external solution, but don't know what else to do. Sometimes they go out in search of a temporary answer that is external, rather than looking internally.

Consider a shopaholic. This person may feel disappointed, sad, or bored. To make themselves feel better temporarily (it is always transient), they shop and spend money – often more than is prudent. This may help through a temporary flood of dopamine (the feel-good neurotransmitter), but it does little to help them learn how to proactively deal with their underlying emotions.

The truth is that in addition to our varied range of emotions, humans are always in some sort of a mood. People have moods, families have moods, communities have moods, companies have moods, countries even have moods. Eras also have moods, such as The Roaring Twenties, The Sixties, etc.

"No matter where we are and no matter what we are doing, we human beings are always in a mood. Ordinarily we don't choose or control our moods – we just find ourselves in them. Once in a particular mood, we become what that mood allows us to be. In this sense, we cannot only say that we have moods, it is also true that our moods have us – we are possessed by our moods." (*On Moods and Emotions*, Dr. Rafael Echeverria, The Newfield Network, 2009.)

It is problematic that many aren't aware that they are *in* a particular mood or emotion. Not appreciating this can make conversations particularly difficult. The right conversation in the wrong mood is the wrong conversation. When people are unaware of the moods that they bring to a conversation, there is an impact on the listener – sometimes it is a big one.

Consider the implications of this observation: If people aren't even aware of what mood or emotion they are in, what can they consciously contribute to a conversation, a team, or the world? How does it affect and influence others when someone is not aware of the state of mind they themselves are in?

What we now know is that we don't have to be victims of our subconscious programs, including our moods.

I have learned that "emotions are basic determinants of what we can and cannot achieve in the domains of work, learning, relationships, sociability, spirituality, etc. Our emotional life is a crucial factor in every sphere of human action." (Echeverria)

In our emotional life "we can draw a distinction between two kinds of phenomena-moods and emotions…in some cases it is difficult to separate one from the other…Emotions are always bound to particular events, and we can normally point to the circumstances that generate them. With emotions, we can identify the events that triggered them. If those events disappear, the emotions that went with them will normally disappear also. Emotions are specific and reactive. Events precede them. With emotions we are often dealing with the way action (or certain events) modifies our horizon of possibilities." (Echeverria)

He continues: "Mood is a different distinction. They are not specific and we normally cannot relate them to particular events. They live in the background from which we act. Moods refer to the emotional states from which action takes place. Like emotions, moods are associated with a horizon of possibilities and with a space of possible actions. However, with moods the relationship between possibilities and action is reversed. We said that emotions have to do with the way action modifies our horizon of possibilities. With moods, on the contrary, we deal with the way a given horizon of possibilities conditions the actions that we take." (Echeverria).

The prevailing belief in our society is that our moods are out of our control; we just find ourselves in them. What is not often appreciated is that a mood is not produced by the "I," but that the "I" is produced by the mood. Who "I" can be at any moment is a reflection of the mood or emotion I am in. By shifting my mood or emotion to one that better serves my desired result, I can extend my capacity for connection and impact. Potential action is limited or enhanced by the mood a person is in.

We have established that moods and emotions can be shifted, but how? The first requirement for shifting a mood is awareness. This means being able to identify and label a mood or emotion. Often this is enough to help shift our conversation just by itself.

It is difficult, if not impossible, to make a big leap from an intensely negative emotion to a strongly positive one. However, small shifts to a better emotion are achievable and produce results. For example, consider moving from anger to discouragement, or from blame to worry, or from contentment to hopefulness (see Scale of Emotions in the appendix). Rather than trying to move from one end of the scale to another (which is not likely to be possible), we *can* go up one rung at a time. The goal is to get closer to the desired feel-good emotion. Over time, our emotional muscle strengthens as we build new neural pathways for emotional resilience.

One of the most powerful techniques I have discovered is to begin with the end in mind. Prior to a challenging conversation, I focus my mind, attention, breath, and feeling on the emotion I would like to have at the end. Often this preview helps lay the groundwork for a stronger outcome and better emotional regulation.

Moods and emotions are not a still life on canvas that is immutable and static. They are more like landscapes in motion, in which there is both ebb and flow. What is even more amazing is that we can *choose and change* our moods and emotions; we don't have to be victims of them. This simple principle will dramatically affect your capacity to influence others.

Action: Choose the Landscape You Want to Inhabit

Discover how to harness moods and emotions for powerful difference.

1. Pick a person with whom you need to have a conversation that could be uncomfortable. What emotion/mood are you in when you imagine that conversation happening?

2. Then ask yourself what emotion/mood would produce a better outcome in this conversation. Imagine yourself there. Take three slow, deep breaths. Visualize yourself already there.

3. How did that feel? What happened?

4. What can you do now that wasn't possible before?

The Body Politic

"The body says what words cannot."
—Martha Graham

Most people who were raised in Western society (and are not athletes or dancers) have an underlying notion that their heads are simply appendages stuck onto their bodies. They believe that what really counts when trying to influence or work with others happens "above the neck." That simply isn't true.

Research has consistently found that the degree to which someone is credible, or to which we trust them, is influenced 55 percent by body language, 38 percent by voice tone and tempo, and 7 percent by spoken words. These studies have been replicated numerous times over three decades, with similar results. The conclusion is that 93 percent of building trust and credibility is communicated *through the body*.

A dull message can be made exciting and even inspirational with voice tone, enthusiasm, energy, and strong, forward-moving posture. Conversely, a brilliant message can be made dull by a speaker whose tone is monotonous and whose body conveys lack of interest and lack of enthusiasm.

Consider some of the great speeches of recent history – the ones that are listened to over and over again. Martin Luther King's "I Have a Dream" speech combines both – magnificent language and rhetoric, with passion, enthusiasm, energy, and forward-moving body posture. The overall effect is memorable, historic, and timeless.

Most lessons in leadership focus on vision, strategies, and action. Very little emphasis is placed on where leadership *lives*. Leadership happens in the *body* as much as in the words that are spoken. What can be done to develop it?

The body of work (no pun intended!) that deals with this area of leadership is called "somatics," from the Greek, meaning "of the body." There is an entire field of coaching that works on helping leaders learn how to "embody" leadership principles.

Consider athletes or musicians. When practicing a technique, the performer doesn't "own" it until it is in their muscle memory. When something has been repeated thoroughly and consistently, it is called "embodiment." Learning without embodiment is short-lived; learning through embodiment is sustainable.

For now, it is enough to create awareness that the body is important to notice and develop. We all have a particular way of entering and exiting conversations. This "coherence" is comprised of breath patterns, posture, stance, visual gaze, expression, etc. Becoming aware of our coherence helps modulate our effectiveness in speech and action.

Elizabeth was preparing for a challenging conversation with her boss. She had a particular disposition in her body (as we all do) that made it difficult for her to muster the appropriate tone and attitude for an effective conversation. We practiced (over Skype!) how she typically stands, sits, and holds herself, paying attention to her gaze, shoulders, stance, and breath. She tried to get the words out, but they did not come. As she practiced, she observed how her body and words did not *allow* for her to have an effective conversation.

After several attempts at shifting, paying careful attention to her body, breath, stance, and expression, the words began to flow more easily. It was a breakthrough moment for her. She realized that the body she inhabited made her desired result difficult, if not impossible. Her awareness, and the shifting of her body that we practiced, eventually allowed her to take effective action. When we followed up in the next session, she indicated that the conversation had indeed gone well. She had gotten what she had requested from her boss (a change of job locale).

Andy had a complex, high-level sales job. He had learned a lot about the features and benefits of his products. What he did not know was how to get in the right body in which to have an effective sales conversation. First he developed awareness of his own body coherence. Then he practiced shifting in and out of different body postures, vocal tones, expressions, moods, and emotions until he arrived at a coherence that felt right for him. Through role-play, he practiced speaking from this new body. As his confidence increased, so did his closing rate.

Action: **Wisdom in the Body**

1. Pick a conversation you need to have in the near future but haven't yet mustered the courage to schedule. Then stand in front of a mirror. Visualize the other person in your mind's eye. Practice observing how you would normally sit, stand, breathe, gaze, and express yourself. Then speak the words you would normally say.

2. How did it feel? How do you think it landed on the listener? Were you effective? If there is room for improvement, try again.

3. Shift your stance, your breath, and your gaze, with a different awareness and intention. Then speak again. Did the words come differently to you? How did it feel? How did it land on the listener?

4. Keep practicing until you embody your new coherence and the words flow effortlessly.

5. Once you have mastered it in the practice arena, it will be natural to do it in the field.

Practice makes perfect.

Breakdown to Breakthrough

"The truth will set you free, but first it will piss you off."
—Gloria Steinem

Have you ever noticed how upsetting and unnerving it can be when someone tells you something about yourself that is spot on, but about which you feel embarrassed or ashamed?

I have learned that the ego (a Latin word meaning "I," often used in English to mean the self, identity, or wanting to protect one's sacred territory at all costs) is a formidable defender. I may feel resentment when someone tells me something about myself that isn't positive, yet is valid. My ego defends and attacks the other as an enemy. This shows up in the form of resistance. We often deny the validity of an observation as the ego fights to preserve its own self-prescribed identity. This battle has little or nothing to do with who we *really* are, but the ego doesn't know that, and wouldn't accept it if it did!

Getting the ego to quiet down is one of the things people learn from coaching that has lasting value. A professional coaching relationship creates a safe space in which people are free to explore their truth. When this takes place in an atmosphere of questions and observations rather than judgment and accusations, people are able to break through to a new understanding of themselves, the situation, or another person. The ego goes on vacation.

A new perspective allows for a range of new potential actions. This is true power, because it frees a person from the cage of their former self. Usually this self is one that has been outgrown, outmoded, and should be outsourced! (By the way, it doesn't even require getting pissed off, although many people will anyway.)

How often have you had a big breakthrough that didn't make you angry at first? How do you respond to experiences that cause you to examine what you are doing repeatedly and produce other-than-positive results? Do you receive the feedback with acceptance, or begrudgingly? If it is the latter, your ego is playing mind games with you.

Action: **Chip off the Old (Ego) Block**

1. Explain a challenging situation or problem to a trusted friend or partner. Request feedback, even if you expect it to be painful to hear at first. Prepare fora it to be painful. Then wait. See what happens when you are prepared and present.

2. How did it feel to you in your body? What emotions arose?

3. Do you see new opportunities that you didn't see before?

4. How does that serve you? How could it serve others?

As a special free reader bonus, I have prepared a Step Up Leader Action Guide to accompany this book. It will assist you in getting the most out of the exercises. To obtain it, simply visit www.StepUpLeader.com and click on "Action Guide."

Light of the Moon

The light of the moon, guide of the night,
Leads us toward a manifold fate,
Our shadows amble solemnly behind us.

Under the mystifying luminescence,
We wander forward, our intentions clear,
Guided by the soft glow.

But soon our shadows split,
Torn asunder by unnatural light,
They lose form, become many.

Soon the simple becomes abstract,
The path once clear becomes forked,
Shadows spring from the tainted source.

They choke us and surround us,
Misleading, misguiding,
Specters of our own device.

The moon becomes shrouded,
This forged light consumes us;
We lose direction and purpose.

Veracity and sanctuary become unknown.
Our path fades,
Lost from our memory.

Light of the moon, guide of the night,
Lead me toward a manifold fate
My shadow, amble solemnly behind me.

Under the mystical luminescence,
Let me march onward, my path clear,
Guided by the warm glow;
A steadfast beacon in the night.

—Jonathan S. Freeman, ©2011

Part |||
Step Up Now!

———✦———

"Management is doing things right;
leadership is doing the right things."

–PETER DRUCKER

Simple Isn't Easy

"Simplicity is the ultimate sophistication."
—LEONARDO DA VINCI

Just because something sounds simple doesn't make it easy. Why is this so?

Human beings are creatures of habit. If everything simple were easy, people would be able to act upon what they have read and understood. Then they would simply do what they learned. This isn't usually the case. Why? Because it's not that easy.

Success from the inside out requires a different framework altogether. It *is* simple. But it is rarely easy. Learning new ways is simple because each individual piece of the puzzle is small and digestible. When built upon and practiced, the new patterns create a symphony that is enthralling, potent, and moving.

The challenge for most people is in the integration. That is where the whole system gets an overhaul and re-boots. This affects thoughts, beliefs, moods, emotions, and the way we speak. Lots of old data that has been archived can be lost along the way. For most of us this is a good thing. What we are left with is that which is essential for our future functioning. Taken in small steps, the process *is* simple, but it is *not* easy.

The difficulty usually lies in wanting to keep outdated modes of operation around for security (just in case), even while embracing the discomfort of outgrowing them. The ego knows only how to hang on, and seeks to maintain the status quo. Like having too much luggage on an exotic vacation, we become weighty. This results in excess baggage charges, which, in this analogy, translates to poor health, poor relationships, and, ultimately, poor performance.

Today's world is the most complex of any time in human history. Technology could simplify and possibly make tasks easier, however, in many ways, modern life owes its complexity to the abundant innovative devices and platforms that influence and run our task-oriented lives.

How much time is spent mastering the latest gadgets? How much time is spent learning and dealing with computers and the information they convey? Is it enhancing the quality of the human experience? Some people would say so. I argue that there is so much complexity in our lives that most people struggle for focus and meaning. Learning to simplify is a step toward that.

I am reminded of when I took a trip to three cities in April, a transitional month at best. For Floridians, there is always the urge to pack more layers than necessary. Before packing I made a decision: Simpler would be easier.

I imagined no waiting in baggage claim and no worry about lost luggage. I took no more or less than was necessary. I got committed to it. I envisioned how much happier I would be with less. The result was that I was able to pack for a week for New York, Nashville, and Chicago (including a formal business event) in one small carry-on bag! (Women, take notice; it is possible!)

By committing to letting go of what I didn't absolutely need, I had room for what was necessary. I felt terrific, light, and yet prepared. People who experience the adage that "less is more" seem to lead happier lives. I think this is a fitting metaphor for lots of things in life.

What is the hardest part? Getting committed to doing something differently. It seems harder, but is really easier than charging through life and suffering through the same unsatisfying consequences.

Try asking, "What is the worst thing that could happen if I simplify?" and then, "What is the *best* thing that might happen?"

What is difficult for you right now that could be made simpler? What makes it difficult?

What have you tried? Who were you being when you tried those things? What were you committed to? What results has that produced?

Where is there opportunity to create simplicity for you or your teams? What are you going to do about it? If you were to accomplish this, what would that be worth?

Reflecting on challenges requires that we look through the lens of simplicity. Often what appears to be complex and overwhelming has a truly simple root, if only we are willing to dig around in the dirt and find it. Just as plants benefit from pruning, so can people and teams.

Tending the garden of simplicity allows the chance for new buds to blossom.

Action: **Simple Gifts**

It can be overwhelming to examine all the ways in which we have complicated our worlds.

1. Pick 3 things that call out for simplicity. What do you want to plant? What do you want to prune? Create three goals.

2. Reflect on why this would be worth working on. What value is created by having made the complex simpler? Then take one small step toward the first goal and see what happens. Follow up with the second, and then the third.

Before you know it, simple will become easy.

Authenticity

"It doesn't happen all at once," said the Skin Horse. "You become. It takes a long time. That's why it doesn't happen often to people who break easily, or have sharp edges, or who have to be carefully kept. Generally, by the time you are Real, most of your hair has been loved off, and your eyes drop out and you get loose in your joints and very shabby. But these things don't matter at all, because once you are Real you can't be ugly, except to people who don't understand."
—THE VELVETEEN RABBIT, BY MARGERY WILLIAMS

What makes great leaders great and memorable? The lengthy list of qualities includes descriptions such as curious, persuasive, visionary, strategic, intelligent, insightful, creative, passionate, driven, dedicated, and committed.

But *how* each leader does this is through authenticity. Books on leadership principles cannot instruct on how to be authentic. Your authentic way is unique to you. Yet we know an authentic leader when we see one. The authentic leader follows a singular compass, trusts intuition, and isn't afraid to be original or out-of-the-box. Authentic power is leadership from within. It is not using force from without, but bringing forth all of yourself. It is about speaking your truth without criticism, blame, or judgment of yourself or others. It is about standing in your own power with clarity.

Much of what we do comes from what we have been told to do, or learned to do out of necessity. But how often does what we do reflect our authenticity? I believe leading authentically involves knowing one's unique talents and gifts and expressing them with passion. Ultimately, we aim to help others discover and express their own talents and gifts. These are the keys to unlocking our true potential.

Childhood is characterized by authenticity. That is one of the reasons it is such an endearing experience for adults to observe. But along the road to becoming adults, the authentic self can get covered up by "should," "had-to," "I'm not good enough," "I am alone," etc.

When commitments are not aligned with authentic passion, there is a heaviness – and often emptiness – in the resulting success. However, when your passions and your commitments are aligned, you live and act authentically.

Is there a longing, talent, or passion that you have buried? Was there a part of you that was discarded long ago because you didn't have time, or had to make money, or for which you didn't get an external reward that you valued?

If you answered yes to any of the above, chances are that a piece of your authentic leadership is missing in action. The reward for recovering it may surprise you. It may show up in renewed energy, drive, and enthusiasm for work and relationships. This translates directly to the impact you can have on others. People will see and feel that you are coming from a place of true power. The energy of authenticity spills over into all forms of communication and action.

The best part is that once you learn to access it on demand, you can help others do so. It is likely that any situation in which you show up as fully authentic will be positively impacted in ways you cannot predict.

Imagine what that could produce.

Action : **Revisiting Authenticity**

1. Take a walk outside for 20 minutes, anywhere where you can be in nature – your backyard or a park is perfect. Bring a pad of paper and a pen, and nothing else. While on the walk, breathe deeply. Notice things you may not have noticed ever before. Bring your focus to the details; see where you are drawn. What calls your attention?

2. The task is to choose an object in nature to which you are drawn. You have 30 minutes to write a short poem about your chosen object. Let your mind go; do not edit or critique the poem in any way. Simply allow whatever comes to you to be written down. Do not quit until you are finished. The length is unimportant. What matters is your full immersion in the process.

3. At the end of the time, your poem is complete. Quit writing. Bring yourself out of the state of flow by standing up and acknowledging your effort.

4. Then read what you have written. Read it just the way you wrote it. Revel in what you have created.

5. In order to complete this exercise, turn to the appendix for final instructions. This is the fun part, but DON'T LOOK until you have done all of the above.

6. How did this expression of your authenticity surprise you?

Go Outside and Play

*"The more I want to get something done,
the less I call it work."*
—Richard Bach

When your mother reminded you to go outside and play, it was a great example of "Mother knows best." She wasn't just trying to get you out from underfoot; she knew instinctively what really was best. It is crucial to go outside in nature, and to play. Combining them at the same time is a win-win!

Play is critical to enhanced human performance because it uses the whole synthetic mind. This harnesses a phenomenal capacity for creative solutions. Play relies on leaving the left-brain logic and accessing the right-brain synthetic, intuitive, and creative capability. When we play, laugh, and experience fun, we allow our full human potential to be expressed. The results can be extraordinary.

At first it may seem counterintuitive. How can it be that if you really want to get something done, you should play? In recent years, play has been taken seriously by thought leaders and executives throughout the world. In *A Whole New Mind,* Daniel Pink writes, "More than fifty European companies, including less-than-zany firms such as Nokia, Daimler-Chrysler, and Alcatel – have brought in consultants in 'Serious Play,' a technique that uses Lego building blocks to train corporate executives. British Airways has even hired its own 'corporate jester' to imbue the airline with a greater sense of fun. And we cannot forget Southwest Airlines, one of the few successful and profitable airlines whose mission statement states: 'People rarely succeed at anything unless they are having fun doing it.'" (p. 187).

How many people in our culture have daily contact with nature? And I don't mean seeing the trees as we breeze down the highway. How many people go outside during the work week and immerse in nature? Man evolved in nature. We are wired to feel our best when we are in our rightful place. In our modern, air-conditioned, plugged-in world, we are often disconnected from the rhythm of the natural world. Our brains and bodies need oxygen and light. We need to immerse ourselves in canopies of green with exposure to natural sunlight. The price we pay for not doing this is high in terms of our physical and mental states, including insomnia, depression, fatigue, and osteoporosis, among others.

Bring play and nature into your life and work. It may seem like a small step, but big things will come of it.

Action: Make Play Your Work

1. Commit to exploring play in one specific area of life or work. Choose an activity in which you will be immersed and joyful – when time will disappear.

2. Try bringing lightness and play into a meeting at work. Consider putting on a piece of upbeat music before a meeting. You can also invite attendees to stand up and move around to the music. This gets the stagnant energy of sitting to move freely. At first, colleagues may snicker and seem uncomfortable. Shortly after this passes, they will be engaged and involved, and forget their initial reluctance. It will feel good, and as their feel-good neurotransmitters rev up, passion for the topic will explode. Just try it once and see. It may become a habit.

3. Commit to getting outside daily for a week, without any electronics, and with the intention of simply being in nature. Pay attention to what you discover while doing the chosen activity. Compare that to what you notice during normal daily activity indoors. Is there a difference? Is it subtle or significant?

Attitude of Gratitude

———

"He is a wise man who does not grieve for the things which he has not, but rejoices for those which he has."
—Epictetus

Gratitude is simple *and* easy. Yet what most people don't know or appreciate is how powerful it is. According to the author of *Simple Abundance*, Sarah Ban Breathnach, "Gratitude is the most passionate transformative force in the cosmos." The simple act of acknowledging gratitude can transform individuals, relationships, organizations, and our world.

By acknowledging what is already working, focus is placed on the *desired* result or outcome, rather than on what is *missing*. A focus on what is missing propels us to create scarcity rather than abundance.

When we do not consciously express gratitude, it affects not only what we can create, but what we can create for others. In a study by the U.S. Chamber of Commerce ("The Balanced Program," 1986), it was shown that appreciation ranked #1 in importance in lists of what is most important to employees, but it was ranked #8 by employers. If gratitude was present, it wasn't expressed. When teams were asked to clarify what they want and need more of from leadership in order to do a better job, money was seldom, if ever, mentioned. ("Enlightened Leadership," p. 132)

The benefits of gratitude are numerous. It is simply good for you. It fills you with a focus on positives – relationships, satisfying work, health, and abundance. We know that what we focus on increases, so the more focus and attention on what is working, the more what is working expands.

Jamie was in the midst of a major upheaval at work and in life. One of the most beneficial practices was the simple act of noticing all that was working well. This practice enhanced her feel-good emotions and bolstered her through the difficult transitions, including relocation to work in another country. Like a boat that is anchored, she was free to move and bobble with the waves of change, but didn't get lost at sea.

What might you be ignoring or missing due to lack of gratitude? Don't dwell on it; just acknowledge that there is a chance to do something different. Make gratitude a foundational element in your world.

Action: **Make Gratitude Sandwiches**

1. Create a gratitude practice that works for you. You may use a computer or a hand-written journal. Daily create a list of 10 things for which you are grateful. The trick is to look for ten *different* things each day, not the same ones. You will begin paying attention to not just the *quality* of what you are grateful for, but also the quantity.

2. Make gratitude a daily practice for one week and notice any changes. As with exercise repetitions, progress is cumulative; only in this case, *there is gain and no pain*!

This practice alone will enhance your experience of life.

Well and Connected

— ❧ —

"The part can never be well unless the whole is well."
—Plato

One of the biggest issues we can face in life is a health challenge. It may not be an actual crisis; instead, it may be a slow, steady progression toward feeling badly, until the feeling is no longer temporary. When this happens in mid-life, many people brush it off, saying, "I am just getting older." They assume this is how they are *supposed* to feel. Nothing could be further from the truth.

Aging is a natural part of the human condition, but aging poorly is not. There is simply no reason why people cannot age feeling healthy, vital, focused, and energetic. Having coached and consulted with many people for whom this was a key concern in their lives, I am going to take a stand for wellness as a value worth having.

The mechanistic, rational mindset that was created by the Scientific Revolution gave rise to a view of the human mind as disconnected from the body. This thinking has predominated in Western concepts of health, much to our detriment. While the Eastern approach considers the mind and body as whole – unified and synergistic – the Western tradition sees the mind and brain as separate from the internal workings of the body. It is as if humans walk around in bodies that are somehow unplugged from the minds and thoughts that control them!

Fortunately, this paradigm is slowly giving way to the more integrated Eastern view of wellness. There is now widespread acknowledgement that what we put in our bodies directly affects how we feel and perform. What we feed our minds also affects how we feel and behave. There is even a Center for Complimentary and Alternative Medicine at the National Institutes of Health, in recognition of the fact that $34 billion is being spent annually by Americans on alternative medicine – as much as for standard therapies.

I believe the focus should be on wellness and prevention. This puts responsibility squarely on each individual to be educated and motivated for health. A self-directed routine consists of appropriate daily exercise, nutrition, and connection with others. *(Younger Next Year,* C. Crowley and H. Lodge, MD, 2004.) The way in which people care for themselves tells a lot about how they can care for others. It is also a predictor of their capacity to sustain performance and enjoyment of life for the long haul.

People cannot control the genes they inherit. However, what those genes express during a lifetime may be influenced by what they are fed. If a person commits to a daily diet of positive, empowering thoughts, food that is as unprocessed as possible, and a body that physically moves a lot, the chances of good health are increased dramatically. Those are odds worth playing.

It sounds so simple. Why do so many people not act on what they know? Education and information can only go so far. Attitudes are gradually changing. Behavior will follow.

Many people lack the self-discipline or support in life to become well and connected. In these situations, an accountability buddy is useful. This is how the weight-loss industry has amassed tremendous success. People like having the support, monitoring, and measured success that comes from working with and through others.

Why bother? Because focus on prevention saves a lot of money in health care expenses down the road; the body breakdowns that cause disease never occur in the first place. Because you will look and feel your best. When that happens, people will be attracted to your energy, and this expands your connection and influence with others. And because the alternative is time-consuming and very expensive.

In order to influence others, we should first have influence over our bodies.

Action: Take Your Vital Signs

1. Commit to assessing your overall health and wellness. Go beyond the standard check-up. Pay attention to how you feel every morning and evening. Compare it to an earlier time in life when you had energy and felt vital. What symptoms call your attention? What could they be indicating? If you don't feel great, don't assume that it's because you are getting older. Often it is a symptom of processes that are not functioning properly and can be restored.

2. Choose a book or CD by a reputable author on a topic of your health that is out of your range of normal reading. Increase your knowledge. What belief did you have that changed as a result of learning?

3. Ask if this could be an opportunity to take care of yourself in a different way than you have in the past. What would that involve? What would the payoff be for your time and investment? Who besides you would benefit?

Dramatic change can seem overwhelming at first. Focus on *one small step* you could take toward improving wellness and whole-body functionality. Just one step. Commit to someone else what you will do and by when. Don't give up. Ask for support and cheerleading. Stay the course. You are on your way!

Connecting Wisdom
to Power

*"The mind can assert anything and pretend it has proved it.
My beliefs I test on my body, on my intuitional consciousness,
and when I get a response there, then I accept."*
—D.H. Lawrence

Why is it so difficult to connect what we know to what we do? There are many possible explanations. I want to focus on one that isn't often found in books on leadership and influence.

Intellectual knowledge can change the world only if it is put into action. How is wisdom connected to power? Can knowledge that is not connected in the body be trusted?

When it comes to influencing and working with others, it is critical to develop a strong ability to connect wisdom to power. Remember that what you say is only a small part of whether or not you are influential. It's more often about the emotions, mood, and the posture you are in when you speak.

Connecting wisdom to action comes through developing a systematic assessment framework. Commitment shapes action. Therefore, identifying the things you care about and your values will affect the conversations you are capable of having. These conversations, if had well, will generate commitments. The final by-product is that your commitment will shape the actions.

This in turn will produce desirable results (summarized from the work of Bob Dunham, Institute for Generative Leadership).

What I often see missing is awareness about how what we care about relates to action. I believe it goes even deeper than that. I think innate wisdom and access to our authentic power is our birthright, and is available to all of us as humans, if only we choose to utilize it.

I am motivated by ancient wisdom rediscovered by a number of credible authors and practitioners in the field of "energy medicine." It is one of the five domains of complementary and alternative medicine identified by the National Institutes of Health. According to Dr. Mehmet Oz, one of the most respected surgeons in the U.S. and director of the Cardiovascular Institute at Columbia University College of Physicians and Surgeons, "The next big frontier in medicine is energy medicine." He is not alone. Dr. Norm Shealy, founding president of the American Holistic Medical Association, stated, "Energy medicine is the future of all medicine." Albert Szent-Gyorgyi, Nobel Laureate in Medicine, stated, "In every culture and in every medical tradition before ours, healing was accomplished by moving energy." (*Energy Medicine*, Donna Eden, p. 27.)

In the twentieth century, Einstein shaped our modern view of the universe around energy. Ancient martial arts practices, including Tai Chi and Chi Gong, and energy practices including Jin Shin Jitsyu, Reiki, and acupuncture, are all based on the same understanding. We have a new way to take charge of health, vitality, and power. It is based on well-understood principles of the energy meridians (fields) that run throughout the human body. These fields, when blocked, disrupted, or "un-hooked," cause distress and disease. However, when they are open, and the energy runs smoothly throughout the body, we experience health, well-being, increased energy, creativity, and productivity.

The trouble is, most people don't know what they don't know, and therefore can't put it to use. My hope is that the emerging field of energy medicine will become an accepted and adjunct approach to Western healing in the near future. In the meantime, it is up to each person to choose how much of this work to integrate into a personal wellness routine. Because it is free and widely available, there is no reason not to try.

An in-depth exploration and demonstration of the effectiveness of these principles can be found in a number of resources, including articles, books, and workshops.

Here's the one thing to remember: Whether you believe or not, you can trust what you experience and feel. Try the following exercise to observe and feel your *chi* – your energy.

Action: Energy Abounds

Moving energy is what keeps humans vital and healthy. Stagnant energy promotes disease.

1. Stand up straight and relax your shoulders, dropping your arms to your sides. Look forward with a soft gaze. Spread your feet hip distance apart and tuck your tail bone. Place your hands two feet apart as if you were holding a big globe in between them. Close your eyes.

    Breathe deeply and slowly, inhaling and exhaling to the count of seven. Take care to inhale from your belly, not your chest. Feel the warmth between your hands. Continue breathing as described for three minutes.

    Slowly move your hands toward each other and then slowly move them away. Do this several times. Notice any pulling or tension as you move your palms toward and away from each other. You may feel a ball of warmth, tingling, or other sensations, but you will no doubt feel something. Really tune in to this feeling. This is your energy field. It is always active, only now you are attending to it.

2. Choose a book or CD that illuminates the concept of energy in the body. Prepare to read or listen with the mind of a learner – of not-knowingness.

3. Practice the Golden Thread meditation found in the appendix.

    Once you have found and connected to your internal power center and can sense its signals, imagine a challenge that you haven't been able to overcome recently. As you breathe into your *dan tien*, observe what happens. Did anything shift for you?

4. Choose an energy practice that you enjoy and will continue. Observe the results over time.

Practice Makes Perfect

"We are what we repeatedly do."
—ARISTOTLE

Practice is where the rubber meets the road. Knowledge can be available. It can even be connected to our innate energy and power. But if we have no consistent practices that embed new learning and distinctions, the journey to becoming a Step Up Leader will lead to a dead end. The human brain naturally goes to its default. And for most people, *default* can mean defeat.

This is also where *care* and *commitment* come in. If you are connected to a deep care and a commitment that is not transient, a practice will be easier to implement. Excellence is a habit. People are always practicing something; why not practice things that are in the service of our cares and commitments?

I work from conscious intention. I believe the world is created and improved (or not) through intention. If we have no intention, we are victims of what swirls around us. Conversely, when we do have intention, we *choose* what we create. Then we are 100 percent responsible for that choice. I can think of no more powerful mind-shift than that from victim toward personal responsibility.

What is the culture of the organization or team you lead? How was it created? Did you go through a thoughtful, energetic, and visionary exercise, or did it just happen on its own? If the answer is the latter, it is worth considering whether the existing culture fosters the achievement of goals and objectives. Is it one in which people are empowered, connected, and valued?

Sadly, this is often not the case in many organizations. The rock under which most consultants and coaches look is labeled "culture." It is here that most interventions must begin. One quick way to take the cultural pulse is to interview stakeholders about their organization and listen for pronouns. If they use "they" a lot more than "we," there is a cultural divide in which people are detached from care and commitment. Likely the results being produced are less than stellar.

As we have already established, we are always practicing something. What is being practiced at work? What systems, formats, styles of meetings, agendas, and communications are being practiced? Are they a reflection of the care, vision, commitment, and values of the organization's leaders? If not, this is the place to begin.

Previous sections have explored how relevant this is to becoming a Step Up Leader. The linchpin of these is practice. I had a teacher who said that when we are in the muck, we do not *ascend* to the level of our competence; rather we *descend* to the level of our practice.

What practices do you have in your own life? Do you have a practice for ensuring you are fully present? Are you listening, curious, and available? Are you aware of your body and its signals? Are you healthy and connected? What is it that you want to practice more of?

If you want to change your physical, mental, or emotional state, there is one universal practice to get there, and upon which everything else depends. *Breath.* So simple it is usually overlooked. Most people live unaware of their breath. Yet it is accessible, convenient, free, effective, and sustainable. Many people are oblivious as to its impact on their health, relationships, and capacity to perform any task in a given moment, no matter what else is going on. In other words, many simply are unaware of how the breath affects their direct experience in the world.

Breath *is* life. Learning to embrace and use it fully is fundamental to becoming a Step Up Leader (and everything else, too). Make it your foundational practice.

Action : **Conscious Practice**

1. Adopt a practice of centering. (See appendix for a sample centering practice.)
    - Set a timer at first, aiming for 3 minutes.
    - Write down three adjectives that describe how you feel before you begin.
    - Do the same after the three minutes is up.
    - Do this for 3 days.

2. Once you see a pattern of improvement, try increasing your timer to 5 minutes, then 10, and ultimately to 20-30 minutes daily. The key is consistency. The body will remember the practice, and the effects are cumulative.

3. When you are in a situation that is difficult, stressful, and challenging, the body will immediately be able to access the memory and feeling from the centering with just a few deep breaths.

This can be done anywhere, anyplace, anytime. It is available to all and it is *free*.

Learning how to breathe and committing to doing so is the best gift you can give yourself. It helps in accessing your full potential, not only for performance, but for satisfaction, connection, and joy.

Trust the Process

"As soon as you trust yourself, you will know how to live."
—Goethe

One of the biggest nuggets of wisdom I have picked up along the bumpy road of life is to trust the process. Even in my darkest moments – the times when I entered the deep night of the soul, when hope was lost – this is the one truth that pulled me forth. Having the courage to do so is where the real gritty work of living happens.

It sometimes takes being knocked about a lot to finally get that our experience of the world consists of processes. We are always in a process. Most of the time, we don't recognize it as such. If we do, however, there is enormous benefit and a lot less suffering.

By reframing our experience to be about a process – at work, at home, or in relationships – we can learn new leadership lessons. From a place of curiosity we can ask, "How did I create this miraculous set of learning circumstances?" "In what ways can they propel me forward to the next place I need to go?" "What have I learned from this?" "Who have been my teachers?"

We can then acknowledge and feel gratitude for all that has occurred. Express gratitude to those who supported and encouraged you. Instead of viewing problems, difficulties, and challenges as burdensome (which they likely are), and viewing yourself as a victim, you can instead move to curiosity (responsibility).

Remember to check that powerful ego at the door. The ego thrives on being able to predict and control. When ego is driving, we are not in our authentic power. We cannot produce new results with the same mindset that created the old ones.

The ability to truly embrace "trust the process" gives true freedom from worry about things that cannot be controlled (most things). It also affords the chance to look at circumstances and people in our lives as part of an odyssey of learning. Suffering is optional. Eliminating expectations of what *should* happen or what we hope will happen is not easy. It requires constant vigilance.

In doing so, you will enjoy the rewards of peace, contentment, and success on your own terms. I can think of no more lasting or worthwhile endeavor for people who influence others.

Action : Trust the Process

1. Look for a challenging situation or problem at work or home. Write a brief 2-3 paragraph description of your problem as you see it.

2. On another sheet of paper, write "Ego on Vacation." Then write a description of the problem from the perspective of trust-the-process thinking.

    Answer the following questions as you do so:
    *   How did I create this miraculous set of learning circumstances?
    *   In what ways can it propel me forward to the next place I need to go?
    *   What have I learned from this?
    *   Who has taught me?
    *   How am I now prepared to move forward in a way that I wasn't before?
    *   What am I grateful for?
    *   To whom am I grateful?

Trusting the process acknowledges that ego plays virtually no role in where growth comes from. And *that* is something to be grateful for.

Intend and Declare

"Try not. Do or do not. There is NO TRY."
—YODA IN *THE EMPIRE STRIKES BACK*

I love this quote. There *is* no try. Try assumes there is no intention. Intention precedes action. If there were intention, it wouldn't be called "try," it would be called "completion."

One of the biggest challenges leaders face is lack of intention among people in their organizations. People are often unclear about their own intentions and therefore send scrambled signals to others. When things don't get done, intention was not present. Getting clear about intention involves the capacity to integrate the material covered in previous chapters. This includes learning to use all of ourselves – our bodies, moods, emotions, and language.

Language is descriptive. But it is not *just* that. With language, the desired future can be created. Without a declaration of goals, it is unlikely it will be accomplished. In addition, while it can be declared, "Our team will exceed previous sales performance by 25 percent," if the culture is disempowered, or the prevailing mood is resignation, what is the likelihood of achieving the result? Not good.

It all works together, in a holistic system. First the leader prepares him or herself by doing the inner work of personal development on the road to self-mastery. This is not to be taken lightly or brushed aside for more "important" work. This is the *real* work of influence and leadership.

Because we are all connected to each other energetically, the individual who exudes a powerful and connected presence will emit that energy to the rest of the team. From that, an environment is established for conversations that can produce the desired future.

It starts with an individual who is committed to a care. The care can be translated into effective communication. Lastly, there must also be an intention to produce results that are meaningful and lasting.

In addition to language, it is also important to focus on the role of emotions and moods. As we explored earlier, we can consciously choose moods and emotions in order to make something happen. Knowing this extends our ability to influence others. There is an appropriate mood or emotion in which to have a conversation or run a meeting. If that is not established at the outset, outcomes will suffer. In order to have the best chance of success, leaders can practice in advance. Over time, we develop enough emotional muscle to enter and exit moods and emotions with agility.

One of the most powerful practices in which to engage is the declaration. Declaring a desire from a place of deep care and vision creates the foundation for the desire to become real. Many people have altered detrimental behaviors by creating an intention and declaring it. Having a declaration witnessed gives it both power and weight. A declaration can be made one-on-one or in a group. The important thing is to allow the time and space for it to happen.

Last, but certainly of equal importance, is accountability. Once a goal has an intention behind it and has been declared, the probability of successful completion increases exponentially if there is a mechanism for accountability.

Consider these statistics from the American Society of Training and Development regarding the probability of successfully completing a goal.

- 10% if you hear an idea
- 25% if you consciously decide to adopt it
- 40% if you decide when you will do it
- 50% if you plan how you will do it
- 65% if you commit to someone else that you will do it
- **95% if you have a specific accountability appointment with the person to whom you have committed!**

Make no mistake. In our wired, information-laden, overcommitted world, having an accountability partner helps bring intentions to fruition.

Action: Intend, Declare, and Observe

1. Choose a situation in which something needed to happen but didn't, and it had an impact on at least one other person. Examine the intention that was lacking. Reflect upon what it was. Why do you suppose it was missing? Once you have brought it to awareness, can you connect intention to action?

2. Choose a goal that has meaning and needs to get done in a specific time-frame. Choose an intention for action. If you are willing, choose a friend or family member to whom you will declare your intention. What happened when you declared it? Observe how it felt. Consider your emotion and your body. What did you notice? Write it down in your journal.

3. Once the goal has been reached, return to what you have written about the experience. What learning has taken place for you? What are the implications for your future planning and actions?

Conclusion

Step Up Now

"What you leave behind is not what is engraved in stone monuments, but what is woven into the lives of others."

–PERICLES

Conclusion

This is the end of what I hope is a beginning. You are part of a sea change of people who acknowledge the gigantic shift taking place on our planet. Organizations and institutions upon which we have constructed our reality are failing. The issues of the day demand that we look at problems differently. It would be foolhardy to attack these problems with the same mindset that created them. Radical new ways of "seeing" are coming forth. As we have examined, these ways are not really new. We already have the required capability to embrace our full potentials. Every one of us can make a choice to step up and do so.

The motto for our time could well be "Adapt and thrive." Throughout history, humans have shown the capacity for constant adaptation. We struggle a lot, even though it is stressful, exhausting, and often does not produce the desired results.

What if there was another way?

What if there was a different way to produce more satisfying conversations, more connected relationships, more trustworthy teams. What if this was available to all? What if people who influence others learned this way and taught it, shared it, and made it the way of the future?

My most sincere hope is that this book supports you and others in your world on the road to evolved leadership. The process I have shared can lead to profound growth and change – the kind of growth that can transform people, organizations, and the fabric of our world.

Congratulations for Stepping Up Now. It doesn't matter where you step onto the track. You may be young, or not so young. You may be a seasoned leader or an emerging leader. We are all walking this journey at our own pace, with our own stepping-on points. Awareness precedes action. But without action, nothing changes. If not now, when?

Thank you for your courage and commitment to Stepping Up NOW.

Epilogue

This book has covered a lot of territory. As a professional coach, this is the domain of learning in which I immerse myself and thrive. However, for someone who is unaccustomed to thinking this way, it can be initially overwhelming.

If all you take away is that you now know what you don't know, the door has been opened for a new chapter of learning. That in and of itself is a victory, and I congratulate you on this important step.

If you have learned that by knocking down your walls of underlying conversations, you can open yourself up to gain innate wisdom, then I congratulate you as well. Only then can you get out of the box of thinking that you don't know what you *truly do know.*

I hope you go beyond the thinking mind of the ego and truly open to unlimited, pure potential.

Influence starts with self-knowledge, and it is a life-long process. In order for change to become a habit, six to twelve months of consistent practice is required. I hope you will go back and revisit each chapter, and practice the exercises contained therein for a week each. See what happens. Continue with those that are challenging. Mastery happens with sustained, conscious practice. Develop new habits, refine, and continue what is working.

While some of us are disciplined and can do this alone, others may benefit from a collaborative relationship with a personal coach. If you are inspired to a path of learning, I invite you to step up and ask for help. This is not a journey that has to be made alone – at least not joyfully. However you grow and develop into your new habits, the benefits will continue for the rest of your life. Likely they will expand to those you influence as well.

Appendix

———◆———

I. Scale of Emotions

Esther and Jerry Hicks have come up with a series of emotions that will help you work from feeling bad to feeling better about whatever you are experiencing. Find where you are emotionally on the scale, and then try to find thoughts that make you feel just a tad bit better about it: Small baby steps toward Joy.

- Joy/Knowledge/Empowerment/Freedom/Love/Appreciation
- Passion
- Enthusiasm/Eagerness/Happiness
- Positive Expectation/Belief
- Optimism
- Hopefulness
- Contentment
- Boredom
- Pessimism
- Frustration/Irritation/Impatience
- Feeling overwhelmed
- Disappointment
- Doubt
- Worry
- Blame
- Discouragement
- Anger
- Revenge
- Hatred/Rage
- Jealousy

- Insecurity/Guilt/Unworthiness
- Fear/Grief/Depression/Despair/Powerlessness

Excerpted from *Ask and It Is Given: Learning To Manifest Your Desires*, by Esther Hicks and Jerry Hicks, Hay House, 2004, p. 114.

II. Poem Completion Exercise from page 103

1. Read your poem for a second time now, substituting the word "I" for the object in nature about which you wrote.

2. What did you observe?

Write about it here:

III. Three-Minute Breathing Space Meditation

Bring yourself into the present moment by consciously choosing an erect and dignified posture.

Close your eyes.

Ask yourself, "What am I experiencing right now in my bodily sensations, my feelings and emotions, and my thoughts?"

Simply acknowledge and accept your experience, especially elements that are uncomfortable or unwanted.

If you find yourself making judgments about your experience, notice what's going on right now.

Bring your attention to your breathing – the rise and fall of each in-breath and out-breath.

As your attention wanders, bring it with kindness and patience back to the breathing.

If you find it helpful, notice the sense of letting go on the out-breath.

The breath is an anchor for bringing you back to the present moment.

Expand the field of awareness around your breathing so that you are aware of your posture and facial expressions, noticing your thoughts, emotions, and what's happening in the world around you.

Let go of any judgments and simply notice what sensations are present in this moment.

Return to the here and now.

Special Offer for Leaders and People Who Influence Others

It is my sincere hope that the ideas in this book have inspired you in some way and that you will choose to take action.

As a way of introducing you to the powerful results that *Step Up Now* offers, I invite you to a complimentary 30-minute "Break Through Your Barriers Strategy Session." Please contact us at Susan@StepUpLeader.com to schedule your session.

CPSIA information can be obtained at www.ICGtesting.com
Printed in the USA
LVOW091053170112

264242LV00004B/1/P